Master Your Emotions

Life Hacks to Retrain Your Brain and Declutter Your Mind to Overcome Depression, Stop Negative Thinking, Manage Anxiety and Control Anger

(2 Books in 1)

By

Charles P. Carlton

Dr. Lee Henton

Copyright © 2020 – Charles P. Carlton & Dr. Lee Henton

No part of this publication may be reproduced, distributed, or transmitted in any form or by any means, including photocopying, recording, or other electronic or mechanical methods, without the prior written permission of the publisher, except in the case of brief quotations embodied in reviews and certain other non-commercial uses permitted by copyright law.

Disclaimer

This publication is designed to provide competent and reliable information regarding the subject matter covered. However, the views expressed in this publication are those of the author alone, and should not be taken as expert instruction or professional advice. The reader is responsible for his or her own actions.

The author hereby disclaims any responsibility or liability whatsoever that is incurred from the use or application of the contents of this publication by the purchaser or reader.

This 2-in-1 Book Consists of Two Parts:

Part I - How to Stop Overthinking

8 Proven, Practical Techniques to End Anxiety, Stop Negative Thinking, Overcome Worrying, and Live a Healthier, Happier Life.

Part II - Cognitive Behavioral Therapy Made Simple

Effective Strategies to Rewire Your Brain and Instantly Overcome Depression, End Anxiety, Manage Anger, and Stop Panic Attacks in its Tracks.

Books By The Same Authors

Books By Charles P. Carlton

How to Stop Overthinking (Change Your Life Series, Book 1)

Cognitive Behavioral Therapy Made Simple (Change Your Life Series, Book 2)

Stop Overthinking and Vagus Nerve Stimulation (2 Books in 1)

Books By Dr. Lee Henton

The Secrets of Vagus Nerve Stimulation

Vagus Nerve Stimulation and CBT Made Simple

(2 Books in 1)

The 5-Minutes DIY Homemade Hand Sanitizer

The 10-Minutes DIY Homemade Face Mask

Homemade Hand Sanitizer and Homemade Face Mask

(2 Books In 1)

The Budget-Friendly Renal Diet Cookbook

Table of Contents

Books By The Same Authors 3

Free Gift 14

About Charles 14

About Lee 17

PART I 18

Introduction 19

Section I – An Introduction to Overthinking and Its Impact on Your Life 23

Chapter 1 24

Let's Get Started 24

    How Our Brain Works When We Overthink? 24

    What Overthinking Is and Isn't? 27

    Causes of Overthinking 29

    Signs You Are Being Controlled by Overthinking 30

    Effects of Overthinking on You 33

    Case Study 35

Practice Test 36

Chapter 2 37

Anxiety, Negative Thought and Worry.................................. 37

    What Triggers These Feelings? 38

    Write Them Down in a Journal.. 42

    Why You Should Write Them Down 43

    Case Study... 44

    Practice Test 46

Section II – Techniques to Stop Overthinking 49

Chapter 3 50

Reflect on the Bright Side of Life Everyday 50

    You Can't Change the Past or Predict the Future: Live in the Present.. 50

    Change the Way You Think: Gratitude Vs. Regret............ 54

    Act with Confidence: Stop Asking "What If"? 56

    Do Away with Negativity and Embrace Positivity 57

    Case Study... 58

    Practice Test 59

Chapter 4 64

Create a To-Do List 64

    How Your Life would be Without a To-Do List 65

    How a To-Do List Helps with Overthinking 66

    Maintain a To-Do List & Stick to it 68

    Case Study 75

    Practice Test 76

Chapter 5 78

Live a Minimalist Lifestyle 78

    What is Minimalism? 78

    Benefits of a Minimalist Lifestyle? 79

    How to Apply Minimalism in Your Everyday Life 80

    Case Study 88

    Practice Test 89

Chapter 6 90

Get Rid of the Past and Bad Relationships 90

    Get Unstuck from Your Ugly Memories 90

How You Can Identify a Bad Relationship 92

Let Go of Certain People 97

Tips to Shake Off Bad Relationships from Your Life 99

Case Study 102

Practice Test 104

Chapter 7 105

Pursue Your Goals 105

Discover Your Vocation 106

What Motivates You? – Your Passions 111

Note Down Your Life Goals 114

Connect Goals to Passions and Prioritize Them 115

Set S.M.A.R.T. Goals 117

How to Set S.M.A.R.T. Goals that WORKS! 119

Case Study 122

Practice Test 123

Chapter 8 125

Practice Mindfulness 125

What is Mindfulness? 125

Why You Need to Practice Mindfulness 126

Effective Techniques for Practicing Mindfulness 128

Case Study 148

Practice Test 149

Chapter 9 150

Be Happy 150

Live Your Best Life: There Is Only One to Live 151

Steps You Can Take to Be Happy 152

Case Study 155

Practice Test 156

Chapter 10 160

Reach Out to Someone 160

Don't be Afraid to Ask for Help 161

Talk to a Physician If Everything Else Fails 164

Case Study 165

Practice Test 165

Conclusion	167
PART II	170
Introduction	171
Charles's Story	176
Section I	179
Understanding Cognitive Behavioral Therapy	179
Chapter 1	180
What is CBT?	180
A Short Trip Down History	183
How Does CBT Work?	186
CBT is About Meanings	187
Where Do These Negative Thoughts Come From?	192
CBT as a Doing Therapy	193
Who Can CBT Help?	195
CBT Principles – What is CBT Like?	197
How Effective is CBT?	199
How is CBT Administered?	204
What Types of CBT Are There?	209

Pros and Cons of CBT 220

Chapter 2 223

What Does CBT Involve? 223

    Step 1: Identifying the Problem and Setting Goals 223

    Step 2: Identifying Core Beliefs About the Problems 225

        What are Core Beliefs? 225
        How Core Beliefs Develop 227
        Identifying Core Beliefs 228

    Step 3: Analyzing Core Beliefs by Identifying Cognitive Distortions 234

        What are Cognitive Distortions? 235
        Types of Cognitive Distortions 236
        Steps to Identifying Cognitive Distortions 241

    Step 4: Cognitive Restructuring or Challenging Your Negative Automatic Thoughts 243

        Finding the Objective Truth About the Thoughts 245
        Making the Restructured Thoughts Habitual 249

    Step 5: Monitor Your Feelings 250

    Exercise 252

Section II 254

Cognitive Behavioral Therapy Strategies 254

- Chapter 3 255
- CBT for Depression 255
  - Understanding Depression 255
  - Symptoms of Depression 256
  - Causes & Diagnosis 257
  - CBT Treatment for Depression 258
    - What Keeps Depression Going? 260
    - *Behavioral Theory of Depression* 261
    - *Cognitive Theory of Depression* 263
    - CBT Technique for Depression 264
      - Behavioral Activation 264
        - Exercise 1 267
        - Exercise 2 268
        - Exercise 3 272
        - Exercise 4 275
      - Mindfulness 278
      - Vagus Nerve Stimulation Therapy 280
- Chapter 4 283
- CBT for Anxiety 283
  - Understanding Anxiety, Worry, and Fear 283
  - Symptoms of Anxiety 285
  - Causes & Diagnosis 285

- CBT Treatment for Anxiety 286
  - Exposure Therapy 289
    - Practicing Exposure Therapy More Effectively 294
      - *Removal of Safety Signals* 301
      - *Multiple Contexts* 302
      - *Retrieval Cues* 303
  - Relaxation Training 304
  - Complementary Therapy for Anxiety 311
  - Panic Attacks 312
    - What Causes Panic Attacks? 314
    - What Keeps Panic Attacks Going? 315
    - Treatment Options for Panic Attacks 317
      - Interoceptive Exposure 318
        - Step One: Pick a Trigger 323
        - Step Two: Create a Fear Hierarchy 323
        - Step Three: Rate the Hierarchy 324
        - Step Four: Starting Exposure 326
        - Step Five: Middle Sessions of Exposure 327
        - Step Six: Ending Exposure 328
        - Exercise 328

Chapter 5 340

CBT for Anger Management 340

  What is Anger? 340

  Angry Thoughts, Behaviors, and Physical Symptoms ... 341

  The Cycle of Anger – How Anger Develops.................... 342

Causes of Anger	343
Cost of Anger	345
Myths & Facts About Anger	346
CBT Treatment for Anger	347
Ellis's A-B-C-D Technique	349
A = Activating Event	349
B = Belief System	349
C = Consequences	350
D = Dispute	350
Exercise	354
Conclusion	357
References	360

Free Gift

In expression of my gratitude for purchasing my book, I am offering you a free copy of my *Bulletproof Self-Esteem* companion guide, proven to boost your self-confidence in **ONE WEEK**.

To have instant access to this gift, type this link http://bit.ly/346qi8P into your web browser, or you can send an email to charlescarltonpublishing@gmail.com, and I would get your copy across to you.

About Charles

Charles P. Carlton, a former consultant with a top big 4 global consulting firm, Ernst & Young and a Fortune 100 best companies to work for is a self-help professional, devoted to showing you the tricks on how to hack your life to get the most out of it by getting things done.

His quest for self-discovery led him to retire from the corporate world to fulfill his life-long goals of being a self-help coach and writer.

He specializes in using a cut-through science-based and personal experience approach in connecting with his audience in areas of emotional intelligence, self-esteem, and self-confidence, self-discovery, communication, personal development, and productivity. This has helped him build successful relationships and connections with his audience.

When not writing, Charles loves reading and exploring

the beauty of nature from where most times he gets many thought-provoking inspirations.

About Lee

Dr. Lee Henton is a US-trained General Practice Doctor from the Johns Hopkins University School of Medicine with additional qualification in nutritional medicine from Iowa State University. He is a certified specialist in dietology and nutrition.

He has extensive years of medical and nutritional experience across general medicine, pediatrics, traumatology, addictions, food nutrition, and diet therapy.

He currently runs a co-established private medical and wellness practice where he operates from. His approach is personalized with each client by combining medical and food nutrition counseling. All advice he provides is at par with his experience, as well as with medical and nutritional concepts. He specializes primarily in men and women's health.

He lives in Minnesota with his wife and two daughters.

PART I

How to Stop Overthinking

8 Proven, Practical Techniques to End Anxiety, Stop Negative Thinking, Overcome Worrying, and Live a Healthier, Happier Life.

Introduction

"You only have control over three things in your life – the thoughts you think, the images you visualize, and the actions your take."

— Jack Canfield

This book contains important information, guidelines, and tips on how to prevent and stop you from overthinking and keep your feelings of anxiety, negative thoughts, and worries at bay.

When the stress and demands of modern life get out of hand, people tend to lose their grip over their thoughts and emotions. Many find it hard to rein in their insecurities and doubts about the situation they are currently in. As a result, they fall victim to the analysis paralysis.

At that point, the person feels stuck in a miserable loop of anxious feelings, negative thoughts, and worries. Overcoming this can be quite a difficult feat to achieve—but it is not impossible.

You are more than your thoughts and emotions. You can break free from your past, be more content with living in the moment and be more receptive to the future. You can also do away with certain feelings or things around your home, workplace and relationships that trigger the anxieties, negative thoughts and worries that besiege you. All of these are possible if you make a conscious decision today to take control of your life and change your course for the better.

To accomplish this feat, you need to make significant changes not only in the way you think but also the way you handle your relationships with yourself and the people around you.

This book shall serve as a guide for you to understand better what overthinking is and what it does to different aspects of your life. Reading through the first section of this book shall also help you recognize and identify the sources of your feelings of anxiety, negative thoughts, and worries.

From this point on, you are encouraged to keep a personal journal by your side as you continue reading in order to document your responses to the practice tests in the succeeding chapters of this book. This is critical because you need to see for yourself how the proposed techniques to stop overthinking can be applied to your personal issues.

As attested by multiple studies conducted over the years by mental health experts, the suggested techniques in the second section of this book can help you reduce—if not totally eliminate—the detrimental effects of overthinking and anxiety in various areas of your life.

These techniques can help you:

- improve how you regard your past, present, and future;
- better manage your daily tasks to avoid analysis paralysis;
- eliminate the non-essential things and toxic people in your life;
- improve your chances of achieving your personal goals and finding happiness; and
- get more comfortable about seeking help and of those who care for you, and from those who are qualified to give you the mental health care that you need.

Do not suffer in silence when you have at your fingertips the possible ways out of your current situation. As an author and public speaker, Ken Poirot once emphasized in his book "Mentor Me," "Right now is the best time to create your tomorrow."

Read each chapter carefully, and reflect on how you can apply the points covered to stop overthinking, anxiety, negative thinking, and worrying.

In the words of Zig Ziglar, "People often say that motivation doesn't last. Well, neither does bathing – that's why we recommend it daily."

Hence to stop overthinking using any of the techniques laid out in this book, you have to apply it continuously.

Thanks for downloading this audiobook. I hope you enjoy it!

Section I – An Introduction to Overthinking and Its Impact on Your Life

Chapter 1

Let's Get Started

"The more you overthink, the less you will understand."

— Habeeb Akande

The path towards a happy and fulfilling life begins with unloading your mind of its unnecessary burdens. Overthinking is considered by many as a natural human behavior. However, this does not mean that you should only accept this without even attempting to counteract its negative effects on the quality of your life.

Before delving deeper into how you can stop yourself from overthinking, you must learn how to recognize the signs that you are engaging in overthinking.

How Our Brain Works When We Overthink?

Overthinking happens when the brain becomes too caught up with certain thoughts, thus causing the person to fail in acting upon the said thoughts. It is essentially a mental state wherein the brain is trapped in a cycle of repeated analysis over the same topic or issue.

As a result, energy is expended unnecessarily, while signs of mental strain begin manifesting in the individual's day-to-day activities and even in one's interactions with other people.

To better demonstrate how the brain works when it is engaged in overthinking, go through the following list of scenarios—some of which may even sound familiar to you:

- You cannot stop thinking about a personal problem or an event that has already transpired. Rather than focus on how to solve your current predicament, you cannot seem to pull yourself away from these thoughts. No matter what you do, your thoughts keep coming back to the problem or the event itself—not what you can do to get yourself out of this situation.

- Something terrible has happened to you. As a result, you cannot seem to stop asking yourself why that has happened to you. You also find yourself ruminating about what would have happened instead if only you had done things a little differently.

- Your mind jumps into the worst conclusions, even without any solid or sound basis at all. It has been occurring to your regularly, so that, by now, the negative thoughts appear to be following some sort of pattern in your head.

- You find yourself obsessing about the tiny details in your day-to-day experiences, especially when it involves interacting with those around you.

- You even come up with dialogues in your head, recreating mentally certain life events where you think you could have done better.

- You assign meaning to every word, thought, and action that sometimes goes beyond what is reasonable and realistic. People also say that you read into things, only to realize later on that they are not worth your time and effort.

If you recognize yourself in any of these scenarios, and if you think that such scenarios happen to you frequently, then you might be falling into the habit of overthinking.

As shown in the examples above, addressing this issue is of the utmost importance. Overthinking is keeping you from moving forward and experiencing new things in life. It is like having your hand-tied with a rope that is attached to a pole. You can only go around in circles around the same thing, over and over again.

What Overthinking Is and Isn't?

Right off the bat, it should be made clear that overthinking is not a form of mental illness. It is, however, a common symptom that can be observed among different types of anxiety disorders.

For example, Ben has been diagnosed with panic disorder. He is prone to overthink about when the next panic attack might happen. If he thinks something might trigger an attack, he cannot help himself but obsess over this possibility. As such, his tendency to overthink these triggers only serves to increase the risk of panic attacks.

You do not have to be suffering from an anxiety disorder to engage in overthinking. This is an all-too-common human experience that happens almost naturally to everyone.

You may feel concerned over what you have said to your friend the last time you talked over the phone. Perhaps, you are worried about an upcoming test or job interview. You might feel a little too conscious about how others perceive you at work. These are just some examples of common scenarios where overthinking is at play.

It should also be noted that there is a distinction between the two forms of overthinking:

- brooding over the past

    Dwelling about the mistakes you have done, and the opportunities you have missed out on can be detrimental to your current happiness and mental state.

- worrying about the future

    The uncertainty of what will happen next can trap a person into a never-ending cycle of "what-ifs" and "should-I's".

Overthinking is also different from introspection. The latter involves gaining personal insights and fresh personal perspectives about a certain matter. You introspect with a clear purpose in mind.

Overthinking, on the other hand, involves negative feelings about things that are usually outside of your control. As such, you will not feel like you have progressed at all after engaging in overthinking.

Causes of Overthinking

There is no single origin or trigger for one to engage in overthinking. It can be born out of genuine worry for one's welfare and those of others. Some overthink as a result of how they have been conditioned to think by their parents, their teachers, and their peers.

Extreme forms of overthinking are believed to be rooted in certain mental and psychological issues that a person is suffering from. These include but are not limited to:

- post-traumatic stress disorder (PTSD);
- panic disorder;
- social anxiety disorder;
- substance-induced anxiety disorder;
- separation anxiety disorder;
- different types of phobias, particularly agoraphobia; and

- physical, mental, and/or emotional trauma.

Linking mental health issues with overthinking, however, is not as straightforward as it may seem. Some experts suggest that overthinking contributes to the decline of one's mental health. However, others are reporting that existing mental health problems can trigger a person to engage in overthinking.

Giving a definitive answer on the actual cause of overthinking, therefore, can get you stuck in a loop. The actual case may also vary from one individual to another.

Rather than ruminate over the exact origin of overthinking, you should focus instead on learning how to assess yourself for signs of overthinking. Through this, you will be able to check if your tendency to overthink is getting out of hand already.

Signs You Are Being Controlled by Overthinking

Much like any human behavior, the effects of overthinking can be described as a dichotomy.

On one end, overthinking may be considered helpful since it allows a person to learn from past experiences and prevent the recurrence of certain mistakes in the future. When used in this way, overthinking can be beneficial in terms of problem solving and decision-making.

The problem begins when these thoughts become excessive, thus creating anxiety, stress, and a sense of fear and dread within the person. At this point, overthinking has gone beyond simply thinking too much about a person or a thing—overthinking has become an obsession that disrupts an individual's capacity to function and interact with other people.

If you are experiencing at least one of the following situations, then it's evident that you are being controlled by overthinking:

- Continually measuring your worth, success, and happiness against the people around you;

- Focusing on the worst possible outcomes whenever you or someone you care for is involved in something risky or dangerous;

- Having trouble in keeping up with and contributing to conversations because you go over your potential responses for too long that either you miss the appropriate timing for your responses, or the conversation itself has already ended;

- Worrying about future activities and task that you must accomplish so much that you feel overwhelmed at just the thought of having to do any of them;

- Repeatedly thinking about personal mistakes and failures from the past, thus preventing you from moving on with your life;

- Repeatedly reliving past trauma, loss, or abusive situation that robs you of your chance to cope with it;

- Failing to calm down your racing thoughts and overwhelming but vague emotions that seemingly manifest out of nowhere.

Please note that the signs of overthinking, as highlighted above, are not exhaustive. However, if you find yourself continuously thinking about certain aspects of your life, or you find yourself in an endless cycle of non-productive thoughts, then that in itself is a sign that you are embroiled in overthinking.

Effects of Overthinking on You

No matter how similar the circumstances are between two people, their respective manner of overthinking would not be the same. As such, the effects of overthinking would be felt differently by each individual.

It has been observed by psychologists, however, that those who cannot control their tendency to overthink suffer from a decreased quality of life. To give you a background on the possible effects of overthinking in your life, here are some common examples of difficulties faced by those who have been identified as chronic over-thinkers:

- Making new friends or keeping the ones they already have can be tough due to their struggles in effectively communicating their thoughts and feelings.

- They find it hard to go out and have fun doing their hobbies because they have already spent their time and energy ruminating about certain matters inside their heads.

- Setting up appointments, or even simply going to the store can be an arduous task for them.

- Taking and exercising full control of their thoughts and emotions seem impossible because their mind is already strained and overworked.

Looking through these points, you can surmise that overthinking can ruin your relationships, isolate you from the rest of the world, and it can increase your risk of developing other serious mental issues, such as depression and anxiety disorder.

The bottom line is that overthinking has wide-reaching effects in almost everything you do and want to do in life. It does not only impose limits on you but also to those who wish to express their support to you. This means that overthinking can create serious problems not only in your personal abilities but also the kind of relationships that you will have.

Currently, there is no single form of treatment that you can adopt to completely relieve yourself of overthinking and its negative effects on you. Perhaps, one day, the mental health community would be able to come up with the ultimate solution for this.

However, this should not stop you from seeking out methods that can help you control your thoughts and eliminate your tendency to overthink. This book shall help you understand and apply the strategies that would work best for you, given the peculiarity of your situation.

Case Study

Amy is a middle-school teacher who frequently found herself worried about what people thought of her as a person, and how people see her worth as a teacher. Whenever she interacted with a parent or a co-teacher, she would usually pause for a second or two to figure out if her words were appropriate or offensive.

At times, Amy would be filled with dread as question upon question began flooding her head. She would attempt to answer all of them, but doing so did not alleviate the stress and discomfort that she felt.

When her overthinking began affecting the quality of her work, Amy decided that it is time to find a way out of the miserable recurring situation. She did not, however, want to settle for a short-term solution.

What Amy wanted was to find a way to stop overthinking for good. She had admitted to herself that something was wrong and that serious steps must be taken as soon as possible. This acknowledgment by itself was a huge step towards her goal.

Practice Test

If you have a similar goal with Amy, you need to take a moment and recognize the effects of overthinking in your life. This will be part of your motivation to pursue your goal to overcome overthinking.

In your personal journal, describe specific incidents in the following key areas of your life where your incessant thoughts have taken over your good sense.

  a. Family

  b. Friendship

  c. Romantic Relationship

  d. Work

  e. Health and Fitness

Then, answer the following questions right after your responses for each area:

- What do you think triggered you to engage in overthinking?
- How did it make you feel at the time?
- How do you feel about that incident now?

Chapter 2

Anxiety, Negative Thought and Worry

"Overthinking can lead to worrying, which leads to anxiety. Anxiety can, at times, be crippling, leave people frozen and unable to act. Overthinking can also lead to depression. Either of these can leave you unable to focus, feeling hopeless, and irritable."

— Brien Blatt

Anxiety is wherein an individual suffers from uncontrollable negative thoughts and excessive feelings of worry. Some people also experience physical symptoms of anxiety, such as chest pains and trembling.

There is no single cause that triggers anxiety, negative thought, or worry. Experts suggest that these feelings originate from the combination of various factors, including genetics and one's external environment.

What is clear at this point is that certain emotions, experiences, and instances can bring out or even worsen the symptoms of anxiety. These factors are referred to as triggers.

What Triggers These Feelings?

Triggers of anxiety, negative thought, and worry vary from one person to another. However, these triggers can be categorized into their probable sources, such as:

- Romantic Relationships

    Relationships are a landmine of potential triggers for anxiety, negative thought, and worry. Even when a couple is just at the start of their relationship, the novelty of being together with another person can put a strain on one's mental and emotional health.

    Having arguments or disagreements with one's partner can be particularly stressful at any point in the relationship. If the couple are not effective communicators, the lack of conflict resolution between them may trigger feelings.

- Family Matters

You cannot choose your family, so even when they make you feel upset or unhappy, it is nearly impossible to cut them off from your life completely. As a result, spending time with them may cause you to feel elevated anxiety levels and increased negative thoughts.

Becoming a parent is typically one of the biggest life milestones that a person can have. Even though it is most exciting, the new responsibilities that this entails can be a trigger for many people.

They may experience doubts about whether or not they will make good parents. Some are also worried about the strain that this will cause to their career, social life, and personal finances.

- Friendships

Much like your romantic relationships, your friendships may trigger your anxiety, especially when you disagree with your friends. You may also begin harboring negative thoughts about them if you fail to communicate with them effectively. Worrying about the future of your friendship with them would then be a common thing, especially when you begin questioning yourself if you should stay friends with them.

- Jobs and Career

  Your current job and career may cause you to feel these things, especially when you do not enjoy what you are doing. Forcing yourself to work for something that is not your true calling can lead you further into a boring, depressing, and unfulfilled life.

- Money

  Financial worries, such as paying off a debt or having to save up money, are commonly felt by people who suffer from these feelings. Unexpected bills and sudden financial instability have also been identified as strong triggers for many individuals.

- Loss

Loss is often associated with intense feelings of sadness, regret, and fear. An individual who has recently experienced the loss of a loved one may feel anxious about what their life would be from then on. They may also have negative thoughts about the circumstances that have led to the said loss. Some may even feel particularly worried that they will never recover from their grief and that they will never feel normal again.

- Trauma

    Personal traumas, whether they are physical, verbal, or sexual, are particularly harrowing experiences for anyone. They tend to have long-lasting effects, especially when the person cannot help but relieve that specific moment in his/her head over and over again.

- Health Issues

    Receiving an unexpected and/or upsetting diagnosis, especially when it pertains to serious chronic illnesses, can trigger one's anxiety, negative thought, and worry.

Because it is deeply personal, the after-effects of receiving such news are usually intensely felt by the individual.

Many people report having more than one trigger for their anxiety, negative thoughts, and worries. Some experience anxiety attacks with no apparent trigger.

Because of this, you must assess yourself and find out what may trigger these feelings within you. By doing so, you will be able to manage them better later on.

Write Them Down in a Journal

An effective strategy to accurately identify your triggers is to start a journal that is dedicated to recording your experiences and feelings related to anxiety, negative thought, and worry.

You do not have to be a skilled writer to keep a journal. As long as you can communicate your thoughts and feelings in written form, then journaling can be an effective personal management tool for you.

Do not worry about grammar rules or spelling. You do not also have to limit yourself to what is socially acceptable or politically correct. This journal is your personal safe space, where you can reveal your true self.

To guide you through this process, here are some valuable tips that you may apply:

- Look for a place where you can write without being distracted or interrupted.
- Try to write in your journal at least once a day.
- When writing about personal trauma, try focusing on your feelings about the incident rather than the details of the said trauma.
- Give yourself time to reflect upon what you have written down.
- Keep your journal away from prying eyes by storing it somewhere secure.

Why You Should Write Them Down

By writing down your experiences and feelings in a journal, you will be able to:

- give yourself more time to process them later on;

- become more objective when it comes to evaluating and dealing with personal matters;

- increase your tolerance for your anxiety triggers and the various stresses of your daily life;

- transform your negative energy into something more open and creative; and

- gain an insight into how you can move forward from these experiences and feelings.

Feeling anxious, having a negative thought, and being worried are natural parts of being human—as long as they happen to you occasionally. However, experiencing these on a chronic level is a sign that there are deeper issues at play here.

If these feelings are starting to affect the quality of your day-to-day life, then you must learn how to accept the fact that you need help, and that you need to act upon this matter soon.

Case Study

Having decided to work on stopping her tendency to overthink, Amy believed that the best way to start this was to document her journey throughout the entire process. In this way, she would be able to look back at her notes and reflect upon the probable strategies she could take.

Since Amy had already identified and recognized the problem, what she wanted to do at this point was to determine the variables that caused her to overthink. She broke her list down into three: anxiety, negative thinking, and worries. Under each, she added the following sub-categories: family, friends, romantic relationship, work, money, and health.

Over two weeks, Amy wrote down in the journal her personal observations about what triggers her overthinking. She took her time to assign each to their corresponding categories.

When she was done, she looked over her list and found out that most of her triggers were work-related. Of these triggers, three recurring themes had emerged. Her confidence as a teacher could be easily shaken by a comment from a colleague. She felt apprehensive whenever parents would approach her to inquire about the behavior of their children within the classroom. An upcoming performance appraisal on her was also worrying her for some time now.

Following Pareto's 80/20 rule—wherein 80% of her problems would be resolved by working on 20% of her list—Amy was now ready to try out potential solutions to her problem with overthinking.

Practice Test

Refer back to the list you have created during the practice test for the previous chapter. Just like what Amy did, identify the triggers for your anxiety, negative thoughts, and worries that caused you to overthink excessively.

Follow this table format in recording your responses:

	Feelings of Anxiety	**Negative Thoughts**	**Worries**
Romantic Relationship			
Family Matters			
Friendship			

Job & Career			
Money			
Loss			
Trauma			
Health			

Next, try to highlight the common themes in your responses. To get the most out of your efforts, it is best to stick to resolving a few issues that can potentially cause a bigger impact on the achievement of your goal.

Recurring Theme #1: _____

Recurring Theme #2: _____

Recurring Theme #3: _____

Section II – Techniques to Stop Overthinking

Chapter 3

Reflect on the Bright Side of Life Everyday

"Once you replace negative thoughts with positive ones, you'll start having positive results."

—Willie Nelson

You Can't Change the Past or Predict the Future: Live in the Present

Living in the present can be a difficult feat to achieve for many. Whether it is through their upbringing or as a result of various environmental factors, most people have been conditioned to dwell about the past and to worry about the future. Even today's technology contributes to one's inability to focus on the present.

Take, for example, the notifications you receive from your phone. You may be fully engrossed in whatever you are doing at the moment. Still, when you hear your phone go off, the mind tends to automatically switch to either a past experience or a future event related to the notification you have received.

Other factors that can keep you from staying in the present include:

- the natural tendency of the mind to edit out the positive aspects of your previous experiences, thus making the past seem more negative than it was; and

- the uncertainty of the current situation you are in, which then generates feelings of anxiety, negative thoughts, and worry.

Many people find it difficult to overcome these elements and start living in the present. Some do not even know what it means to be in the present. They cannot imagine how it feels like to be free from their ruminations about the past, and their apprehensions about the future. Most of the time, they simply do not have enough personal will to focus on what is currently happening to them.

Fortunately, there are various ways to get over the challenges of being in the here and now. Through the right mindset and a positive attitude, you can start living in the present and make better life choices.

When you live in acceptance of what has already happened, and what will come to pass, then you will begin seeing things for what they truly are. You will be able to forgive yourself and others for the mistakes that have been made in the past. You will also be able to free yourself from feelings of anxiety and worry about the things that may come your way.

Let me share my personal experience on this subject!

So, it just happens that I had made at some point in my life, quite too many financial mistakes and bad financial investments that did cost me some huge chunk of my savings for the supposed pleasant life I looked forward to living. Not once, not twice, not even thrice. Under these circumstances, I should have typically read the signs on the wall, right? and know what investment is good and bad, but duh! *(laughs)*, I kept sinking in much money in more investments, but this time around, in a bid to recover my previous financial losses. However, I ended up losing more and more. At a point, I lost it and went into bouts of anxiety, negative thoughts, and worries about the mess I created in my finances and how I should have known better after the initial three losses incurred. I would overthink what would become of my financial status, especially at the point of my life where I was somewhat out of a job. I was scared, unhappy, and angry every other day I lived. This feeling went on for as long as I could remember, and then, on one Tuesday morning, I laid woken right on my bed and looked up, gazing into the ceiling before me, and I asked myself, a life-changing question.

"How has my overthinking of the past financial mistakes, what I could have done differently, and what the life I hoped to live in the future has helped me achieve?".

I decided that I was going to leave the past mistakes where it belongs, "the past"— I was going to focus on living in the present by making the most out of it— and that I wasn't going to beat myself up about what the future holds. Consciously deciding on this gave me a great sense of relief and peace.

No matter how much we try, we can't change the past simply because it is out of our control, and no matter how we wish we could predict the future, we simply can't because the universe operates on its terms and conditions. So then, the obvious choice you can make, one which you have control of is to live in the moment and enjoy what each day brings. It sure helps.

Change the Way You Think: Gratitude Vs. Regret

Everyone has felt regret at different points in life. You may have gotten over them by now, but you have

surely experienced how heavy regrets can be.

Regret can be something you have done—whether deliberately or unintentionally—that have hurt yourself or somebody else. You may also feel regret after making a snap decision that resulted in something less favorable than it should have been had you only taken your time.

Having regrets is a normal human experience. Obsessing over them, however, is not healthy nor productive, and would most likely result to overthinking which in turn would produce bouts of anxiety, negative thoughts and worry. There is no way to go back in time and change the circumstances that have led to those regrets. The only way to go is forward.

To overcome a regretful mindset, you must learn how to adapt and apply gratitude in your life. Rather than ruminating about what has happened and what could have been, you should switch your attention to the good things that are happening in your life.

Changing the way you think is not something you can do half-heartedly. You must learn how to practice gratitude whichever way you can. You can do it by literally keeping track of the fortunate instances you have experienced in life. Others find the habit of writing down positive things to help keep them grateful, especially during tough times.

You can even take this further by being thankful for the lessons you have gained from your past, no matter how painful or hard they are. Be thankful that you have managed to live through them, and you have then been given the opportunity to learn from your past mistakes. You are now a step closer to enlightenment and becoming a better version of you.

Once you have chosen to adopt a grateful mindset fully, then you will be able to:

- feel contentment about the blessings in your life;
- gain an optimistic point of view;
- better appreciate the people around you;
- find ways to help those in need; and
- have a higher level of self-awareness.

Take note that successfully overcoming your regrets does not happen overnight. You must be patient with yourself, and continually practice applying gratitude in all aspects of your life. The more you practice it, the easier it becomes to access a grateful mindset, even during trying times.

Act with Confidence: Stop Asking "What If"?

Torturing yourself with the question "what if" gives you nothing but unnecessary feelings of anxiety, negative thoughts, and worry. There is no way to know for sure what will exactly happen by choosing to act in a certain way. It is a waste of time and energy to think about the uncontrollable aspects of the future.

More often than not, obsessing over the possible outcomes of your actions will only make you feel upset. Having no definite answer since there is an endless number of possibilities can be particularly unsettling.

To stop asking yourself this question, you must:

- focus on the here and now of the situation;
- identify the things that are within your control; and

- think of each situation as an opportunity to learn.

If you do end up acting upon the wrong decision, the only healthy thing to do is to learn from it and move on. Do not let your mistake define your present and what your future would become.

Reallocate the time and energy you would have used in overthinking about the what-ifs of the situation into something more productive. Use that as a motivation to make better decisions the next time you are facing a similar circumstance. Remember, you can take more control over your thoughts and actions if you would simply believe you can do so.

Do Away with Negativity and Embrace Positivity

There are days when nothing seems to go your way. The moment you wake up, you just know everything that can go wrong will go wrong.

Since you are already expecting it, any disappointment that comes your way further strengthens the negative vibes that you are feeling. When this happens over and over again, those vibes solidify into a perennial negative mindset.

If this scenario sounds familiar to you, then know that you have the option to turn things around for the better. You are in control, and you can choose how you are going to approach important matters in your life.

From here, you can start nurturing a positive mindset that is centered around your personal growth and development. You can reframe your outlook in life, thus giving you hope and motivation to overcome the challenges that may come your way.

It should be noted that you should actively work on embracing positivity. Once you have acknowledged that you have the right to be happy and that you are ultimately responsible for your happiness, you may then proceed to apply this positive mindset in your day to day life, and the achievement of your goals.

Case Study

While searching for effective strategies to combat the negative effects of overthinking and anxiety, Amy stumbled upon the various research works conducted on the field of positive psychology. There, she learned that she had to let go of what had happened to her in the past to give space to a more positive present and future. She had also realized that her regrets about missed opportunities back in her days at the university were bogging her down.

While writing down these reflections in her journal, Amy decided to apply some of the techniques she had read about. First, she made a list of the blessings and things she feels grateful for in her life. Then, she copied each on a separate sticky note.

Since the most of her triggers were work-related, she posted the said sticky notes on a board beside her work desk. In that way, she could easily see them whenever she needed a boost.

Over a week, she recorded in her journal how she felt after a few minutes of staying at her work desk. She had noted small but steady increments in her mood day by day. There was one positive fluctuation, however, when she took the time to read through some of the posted notes.

Given her observations, Amy resolved to make a habit of counting her blessings and remind herself of what she was thankful for.

Practice Test

Create your gratitude list based on the people, things, and life events that you feel thankful for in different aspects of your life. Follow this suggested format so that you can use this list to answer the following questions.

- Romantic Relationship

    a. _____

    b. _____

    c. _____

    d. _____

    e. _____

- Family

    a. _____

    b. _____

    c. _____

    d. _____

    e. _____

- Friendship

    a. _____

b. _____

  c. _____

  d. _____

  e. _____

- Job & Career

  a. _____

  b. _____

  c. _____

  d. _____

  e. _____

- Money

  a. _____

  b. _____

  c. _____

  d. _____

  e. _____

- Health

    a. _____
    b. _____
    c. _____
    d. _____
    e. _____

- Others

    a. _____
    b. _____
    c. _____
    d. _____
    e. _____

Based on your responses, answer the following questions:

- How do you feel after writing down this list?

- Which category/categories contains the most number of listed items? Describe how you feel about that particular aspect of your life.

- Which category/categories contains the least number of listed items? Describe how you feel about that particular aspect of your life.

- Do you possess a more positive or more negative outlook in life? Why do you think so?

Chapter 4

Create a To-Do List

"Each day, I will accomplish one thing on my to-do list."

— Lailah Gifty Akita

A to-do list is one of the most basic, yet easily overlooked, task management tool at anyone's disposal. Essentially, a to-do list contains information about what you should be doing, how it should be done, and when it must be done.

The principle behind a to-do list is quite simple. It has also been around for so long. However, no matter how simple it is, the problem with a to-do list is that people tend to forget about them eventually.

Some find it too simple that they think it is not effective in serving its purpose. Others recognize the importance and merits of a to-do list, but they lack the discipline in maintaining one in the long run.

To better illustrate to you why you should create and keep a to-do list, the next section covers the effects of having no to-do list in your day-to-day life.

How Your Life would be Without a To-Do List

Life, by nature, is chaotic in itself. This is further complicated by the demands and complexities of the modern way of living.

With the mountain of tasks that you must accomplish day by day, things can quickly become overwhelming. When this builds up, the amount of stress in your life will increase exponentially.

Many experts recommend the usage of a to-do list to manage one's activities and responsibilities better. However, some people find it hard to pick this up as a habit.

Studies show that without a to-do list, an individual's level of productivity significantly drops down. You may also experience the following scenarios when you do not create a to-do list of your own:

- jumping from one task to another, thus decreasing your efficiency in finishing up your tasks;

- missing out on important deadlines because you forgot that you have to do it in the first place;

- being vulnerable to potential distractions around you;

- struggling to achieve a balance between your home life, your work life, and social life, among others;

- having no sense of direction at all especially when it comes to what you should be doing next; and

- lacking the feeling of accomplishment by the end of the day.

To resolve these problems, you should try incorporating the creation of a to-do list in your daily habits.

How a To-Do List Helps with Overthinking

One of the most significant negative effects of overthinking is analysis paralysis. This means that you become stuck in your mind, mulling over the same issue over and over again, without anything to show for it. This then leaves you with little to no time and energy to act and carry out your other tasks.

A to-do list can help you overcome this by keeping you focused and on track with what truly matters. Aside from boosting your productivity, it may also be beneficial to you in psychological terms.

According to researchers, a to-do list can:

- give you the motivation to get things done;
- prevents you from being distracted by your irrelevant thoughts and other unnecessary elements from your environment;
- prevents you from doing unnecessary repetitive behaviors;
- break down complicated tasks that may bring about feelings of anxiety and worry about failing to accomplish the said task;
- improve your pacing, and therefore decrease your stress level;

- relieve you of the pressure to finish everything all at once; and
- relieve you of the worry that you have forgotten to do something important.

Ultimately, a to-do list can also make you feel happy and satisfied. A listing with all the items crossed out serves as proof that your day has been quite productive. You will be able to fight off any feelings of doubt, especially those of self-worth and self-confidence. As such, your mind will have no reason to devolve into an endless spiral of anxiety, negative thoughts, and worry.

Maintain a To-Do List & Stick to it

Many people who do not—and can not—maintain a to-do list view it as a burden. They think of it as a list of chores to do and deadlines to meet. Over time, this perception prevents them from making a habit out of creating and managing a to-do list.

Some people are natural at keeping things organized and on track. However, for those who are not born or conditioned to do so, here are some effective tips that will allow you to maintain and stick to your to-do list:

- Associate your to-do list with positive thoughts and feelings.

  This is the first thing you must do to incorporate a to-do list in your daily life successfully. Remind yourself of the practical benefits of keeping one. Try to recall how good it feels whenever you get to cross something off your list. By doing this, your brain will be conditioned to put things in your to-do list to get it done and crossed off.

- Write the list for the benefit of the future.

  You might not immediately realize the advantages of maintaining a good to-do list, but your future self would appreciate your efforts. No matter how good you are at remembering things, life may throw you a curveball at any moment.

  This may leave you scrambling for direction and information. A to-do list that contains all the important details that you must keep in mind would be a lifeline during those challenging times.

- Categorize the items on your list, depending on their importance and your personal preference.

Many people skip the process of categorizing the items on the to-do list. This is an important step to make because it improves your chances of getting things done. Through this, you would be able to prioritize your tasks better.

One way to categorize your list is by arranging it according to what must be done, and what would be nice to do if you have the extra time. By doing so, you would not miss out on the all-too-important deadlines in your life. It will also remind you of the things you can do with your time, thus saving you from having to rack your head for something to do.

- Accept the fact that to-do lists are changeable.

  Remember, a to-do list is only a tool. Its contents are not rules or demands that you must follow at all costs. Sometimes, you have to change the items in your list to suit your current needs.

  Starting anew is perfectly alright. It shows that you flexible enough to roll with the punches. By learning how to adjust yourself and your to-do list, you will be able to better deal with the stress and anxiety triggers that may come your way.

- Treat your to-do list as a symbol of your accomplishments.

  Conquering your to-do list requires a lot of time and effort. Therefore, it is normal to feel proud about finishing a task in your to-do list.

  Similar to assigning positive feelings to your list, thinking of it as a record of your wins for the day will help you stick to this habit.

  This will also do wonders for your mental health. Anxiety, negative thoughts, and worries will have little to no place left in your head when it is filled with your accomplishments for the day.

Now that you understand the importance of having a to-do list and how maintaining one can drastically simplify any feelings of anxiety, negative thoughts and worries you could have, it is also important to know how to create an effective to-do list.

Creating an Effective To-Do List

Some rush through the process of creating a list, thus giving them a one-word outline that vaguely describes what they must do. As a result, they cannot follow through the listed tasks, which then leaves them an impression that to-do lists simply do not work for them.

To help you write an effective to-do list that WORKS for you, follow these quick and easy steps:

1. **List down three tasks, at most.**

   A shorter list containing the most important tasks that you must accomplish would allow you to get a sense of accomplishment by the end of the day.

2. **Make each task actionable.**

   You can do this by using an active voice rather than simply indicating the outcome that you want to accomplish. For example, instead of listing down "detergent" in your list, you should write "go to the grocery store and buy detergent."

   The first part of the suggested statement may sound obvious and unnecessary to you. However, keep in mind that the more complicated the task, the more helpful it is to include these small details into your to-do list.

3. **Assign the priority level for each task.**

   You may ask yourself which of these tasks would make you feel most accomplished. Your answer would then have to go to the top of your to-do list (priority list) with a "high", "mid", or "low" label depending on their relative urgency to you.

4. **Write down the rest of your tasks in a separate sheet or file (overflow list).**

   They should go to another queue, so that you can focus on what matters. Since the top three tasks are considered as significant items, they may also take up a lot of your time. Therefore, keeping the other tasks in a different list would keep you from feeling overwhelmed.

   Ideally, you should store this where it is accessible but away from your sight. This would enable you to refer to the overflow list when you have run out of things to do in your priority list.

5. **Make your priority to-do list visible.**

   You may transfer them in small post-it notes that you can stick in a location that you frequently see or go to, such as the refrigerator door. If you prefer to add more details, you may opt to use index cards instead.

6. **View each task one at a time.**

   Many people feel overwhelmed whenever they see a list of things that they must do. To prevent this from turning into a negative feeling, you can impose viewing limits upon yourself.

   There are certain task management apps, such as the "Todoist" and "Omnifocus", that allow their users this viewing option. However, if you are using post-it notes or index cards, then you can just simply stack them over one another so that you can only see the topmost item in your list.

7. **Record the status of your task**

   Recording the status of your task whether accomplished or not makes you accountable. It makes you have a deeper reflection on the position of your commitment to fulfilling your tasks for the day. It makes you ponder on how you can improve on your level of accomplishment and also gives you a sense of refocus to ensuring that unaccomplished tasks are executed and taken off your to-do list as quickly as possible.

Case Study

Despite Amy's effort to research about potential strategies, she felt like she was not making much progress on this. Her main problem was that due to the overwhelming amount of information she had amassed, she was not entirely sure where to start. She also kept jumping from one strategy to another, thus leaving her a pile of unfinished tasks.

To resolve this, Amy followed the advice of her best friend, Danny, to make a to-do list. Since this is incredibly personal, she downloaded a task management app on her phone, where she can privately store her to-do list.

Amy also decided to create one list per recurring issue that she had identified earlier. In that way, she would know if she had done any action in resolving the said issues. Using the app, she assigned the priority levels and set up reminders that will notify her now and then of what she should be doing.

After a week of using the to-do list, Amy finally felt like she was back on track with her personal project to stop overthinking.

Practice Test

Create your own to-do list for each day or as required using the format below. For the "Priority Level", assign each task a "high", "mid", or "low" label depending on their relative urgency to you.

Use the "Status" column the following day to indicate whether or not you have accomplished your tasks.

Task #	Task	Priority Level	Status

Carry out the task listed in the table you have made. On the following day, answer the following questions based on your experience:

- How many tasks have you accomplished?

- How did you feel when you accomplished a task?
- How many tasks have you not accomplished?
- How do you feel now that you have not accomplished a task from yesterday?
- How do you think you can improve upon your level of accomplishment?

Chapter 5

Live a Minimalist Lifestyle

"The secret of happiness, you see, is not found in seeking more, but in developing the capacity to enjoy less."

—Socrates

What is Minimalism?

Many people associate minimalism with stark white walls and sparsely furnished rooms. However, that aspect is only one aspect of minimalism—one that is done out of the personal preference of the individual.

Lifestyle experts consider minimalism as a way of life that encourages intentionality, simplicity, and clarity among its followers. Its applications are not only limited to the home, but also other important aspects of life, such as your relationships, career, and digital presence.

Minimalism promotes the recognition of the value of the things you keep and the people you interact with.

As a result, anything that does not fit with your goals and purpose in life is discarded or avoided.

Some people misunderstand minimalism by equating "less" with "none." However, this assumption does not align with the basic principles of this movement. Minimalists are allowed to keep things with sentimental value—even though the said things do not serve any other function whatsoever. As long as something brings value to your life, then you may choose to keep it with you.

Embracing minimalism may require significant changes in your current lifestyle. It is well worth doing, given the benefits, it brings, especially for the wellness of your mental health.

Benefits of a Minimalist Lifestyle?

A minimalist lifestyle is considered as the complete opposite of a life riddled with anxiety.

Anxiety is characterized by excessive worrying, overthinking, and high levels of stress. As a result, you will lose focus on what you should be doing. You become easily overwhelmed by your responsibilities, negative thoughts, and fears.

This condition is further exacerbated by a cluttered space. It is difficult to relax and be calm in an environment filled with unnecessary and disorganized things.

On the other hand, minimalism promotes a clear focus on the things that matter in life. Therefore, you may be able to pursue your goals and function well without giving in to the distractions around you.

When you adopt a minimalist lifestyle, you will gradually be freed from the rush and demands of the modern way of living. Since you have to disengage from non-value adding activities, you will have more time to pursue the things that you want to do in your life. You may also use this time to improve the quality of relationships that you have with the people around you.

To reap the benefits of a minimalist life, you need to learn how you can incorporate its principles into various aspects of your life. To guide you through this, given below are the essential tips for beginners.

How to Apply Minimalism in Your Everyday Life

- Home

The goal when reducing the clutter in your home is to assess whether or not an item adds value to your home or has a value to you. Based on your assessment, you may categorize each item according to these categories:

- o For keeping
- o For donation
- o For selling
- o For disposal

Saving an item may mean that it has practical use in your home, or that it has a sentimental value that makes you want to cherish it. An item may also possess both qualities, like a set of hand towels that you have received as a gift from your mother.

If you choose to donate an item, it is best to select a local organization that helps individuals who may find a use for your item. You may also consider donating them to thrift stores that would sell the item to those in need.

Selling can either be done by holding a garage sale, or by posting it on online platforms.

Through this, you will be able to convert the item into something more useful to you.

Disposing of the items that have no use or no sentimental value to you can be beneficial for your overall wellness. You would typically feel a sense of accomplishment because you have attained your goal for this project. The process itself can also relieve you of stress and anxiety since the items may be contributing to the negative thoughts and feelings that you have.

For this process to be institutionalized within you, it is advisable to make a schedule for this. How frequent you do it depends on your preference. What matters is that you will allot a specific time dedicated to this activity.

- Workplace

   Since your personal space at work is most likely limited only to your workstation, then this is the best starting point. You may begin by removing all items from your desk. Wipe it clean, and remove any stains, if there are any.

   Then, sort through your stuff by assigning their respective value to your work. Anything that does not serve any purpose to your current responsibilities and projects should either be archived somewhere else or discarded properly.

Once you are done, rearrange the things you have identified as essential back on your desk. Dispose of any remaining clutter to keep your workspace clean and organized.

To prevent you from overthinking, which things will be kept and which will be discarded, set a timer to 15 minutes only. By sticking to the time limit, your mind will be forced to focus on your objectives.

You may repeat this process every week, or whenever you notice clutter piling up in your workspace again.

- Relationships (Romantic & Friendship)

By applying minimalism to your relationships, you will be able to finally move on from the painful experiences you have had in the past and replace that emptied space with good memories that you will have with your new relationships.

To do this, you must first let go of the past. Acknowledge the mistakes that you have made and move forward while bringing along only the lessons you have learned from them.

Then, apply the principle of "less is more" in terms of determining the relationships that you want to add and keep in your life. You don't need hundreds of acquaintances when you can have a handful of true friends who have your back no matter what.

- Digital Life

    Digital minimalism aims to ensure that our use of technology is intentional and kept at the barest minimum. It is motivated by the fact that intentionally doing away with digital noise, and optimizing your use of the available digital tools that are important, can tremendously improve the quality of your life.

    In this technologically advanced age, we often get bogged down with lots of digital distractions, which could come in different forms that most times cause us to lose ourselves in the process, leading to an out of control feeling of anxieties, negative thoughts and worries.

To have better control of your thoughts, there are several digital minimalist practices that you can apply to simplify your digital and online presence to gain better control of your thoughts, a few of which I would touch on below.

- Simplifying your Digital Files and Emails

Clutter can also pile up in your files and emails. This can come in various forms, such as an overflowing inbox, or a maxed-out hard drive. Much like physical clutter, these can contribute to your stress level and anxiety.

To apply minimalism to your files and emails, you first have to go through each of your digital files and emails. Delete those that are not important, and categorize those that you will keep. To prevent the mistake of deleting an important file, it is best to save a back-up copy before commencing this activity.

It is easy to put this off for another time, especially since it is not as pressing as your other tasks. However, you have to give time for this, even in small 10-minute bursts throughout the week. By doing this, you will be able to clean up your files and rearrange them in an orderly fashion.

Scheduling this activity regularly would also keep everything manageable for a longer period. A once-a-week backup and cleanup of your digital files and emails should be sufficient enough in most cases.

- Simplifying Usage of Social Media

Social media is a wonderful yet noisy place, which attributes to one of the major sources of anxiety, negative thoughts, and worries. If you fail to use it wisely, you would most likely be caught up with the clutter it freely gives and ending up in rabbit holes. For example, people who visit Facebook regularly may experience a change of mood to somewhat negative because you get caught up comparing your life with others you see on Facebook who appear successful, beautiful, and happy.

Although social media has helped in making useful professional connections easier such as

LinkedIn, even at that, you might feel professional anxiety when your peers are making waves in their careers and life in general. Hence, it has become increasingly important to minimize your usage of social media to keep your mental health in check.

To keep your thoughts in check, you need to realize that most people who put up great posts on social media have a normal life just like you but only put the good stuff they want you to see, leaving out the not so good things about their lives— some people put up a "fake it until you make it" post. The bottom line here is social media isn't real life, and you simply have to take whatever you see on social media with little or better still no interest and go out there in the real world and live your best life.

You can also control what you see on social media. Simply unfriend and unfollow anyone whose posts or feeds are both distracting and of no value to your life. If this still doesn't help, then deactivate your social media accounts and delete the social media app from your phone. Trust me; you'll survive only if you make it an intentional decision. Your mental health comes first before any other thing.

Case Study

One of the potential strategies that Amy was considering is adopting a minimalistic lifestyle. Before trying it out, she decided to analyze first how she could apply it to the key areas in her life. Given that her triggers are work-related, she opted to focus on that during this trial phase.

Booting up her work laptop, Amy looked through her files and inbox to check their current status. She frequently did not take the time to sort her documents into the right folders properly. Most of them are just there on her desktop. Her inbox was also filled with unread messages from the various sites that she had subscribed to while she was conducting her research.

Applying the principles of minimalism, Amy sorted, deleted, and categorized all of her files and emails, over one week. She also unsubscribed from any previously joined mailing list she no longer needed that contributed to the overflow in her inbox. By the end of it, she felt a sense of calm whenever she saw how organized her files and emails are.

To maintain this, she added in her to-do list a regular cleanup of both her files and inbox.

Practice Test

Try to apply the guidelines given earlier in this chapter regarding the reduction of clutter in your digital files. Makes sure to save a backup of your files and emails first before proceeding with this exercise.

After doing this activity, answer the following questions based on your experience:

- How do you feel after completing this exercise?

    Do you think you can create a habit out of this? Why or why not?

Chapter 6

Get Rid of the Past and Bad Relationships

"Letting go doesn't mean that you don't care about someone anymore. It's just realizing that the only person you really have control over is yourself."

— Deborah Reber

Get Unstuck from Your Ugly Memories

Letting go of the past is easier said than done. However, people are hardwired to hold on to things that feel familiar and comforting. Even when it is essentially based on a negative experience, the human mind tends to romanticize certain aspects of the past.

Some people use their past as an excuse and basis for the decisions they are making now. For example, Glenn had a nasty argument with his former high school friend, Karen. As a result, he decided to burn bridges between her and his other friends in high school, thinking that he had already outgrown them at this point in his life.

This example shows how dangerous the past can be to your present and future. The kind of memories you keep shapes your current path and controls the direction that you are heading to.

Therefore, if you keep holding on to the past, especially to your negative experiences, then expect misery and loneliness to be your perennial companions in life.

To realign your focus towards a more optimistic and fulfilling future, then you have to learn how to let go of your past. This involves all the mistakes you have made, and the bad decisions that continue to haunt you.

Past relationships are usually riddled with mistakes and bad decisions. Yet, they are often the hardest things to let go of from your past. No matter how badly it ended, people tend to hold on to the experiences and feelings they have had with the former partners.

To free yourself from these memories, you have to take a proactive approach. Time will not simply heal your wounds if you keep prodding at them. You need to actively find ways to sever the ties that keep you from accepting the past and moving on.

Acknowledging the existence of a problem triggers the need for a solution. Therefore, the first step you need to take is recognizing a bad relationship for what it is.

How You Can Identify a Bad Relationship

Many people find it hard to recognize if they are in a bad relationship or not. Some have been conditioned to accept unhealthy expressions of love as normal, while others make up excuses for their partner's flaws. People who feel like they are too deep in their relationship tend to turn a blind on the glaring signs around them.

Some relationship issues can be passed off as mere quirks that you can learn to accept overtime. However, there are serious relationship problems that can make or break a couple.

To help you identify the red flags of a bad relationship, here is a list of the signs that you need to look out for:

- You feel like you have to change yourself to better suit your partner.

    It is perfectly alright to try out new hobbies that your partner has, just to see if you would also enjoy doing them. It is also fine to switch things up in your life, for the benefit of your growth and development as a person.

This becomes a serious issue if you feel like the current version of you would not meet the expectations of your partner. If you find yourself changing the way you normally dress, or if you start changing your opinions and values according to your partner's thoughts and feelings, then your relationship with him/her has crossed the line of what is acceptable and what is not.

- You have to defend your partner to family members and friends.

Not everyone has to like your partner, but it is alarming when no one among your family and friends like him/her. If they are all uncomfortable with your relationship, then it may be a sign that you have to take a better look at it.

- Your partner frequently criticizes you, even when said criticism had been expressed as a joke.

By doing this, your partner is putting you down in a passive-aggressive manner. Over time, these criticisms will chip away your self-confidence, which can then lead to feelings of anxiety, negative thoughts, and worries about the future of your relationship with him/her.

- You always find yourself wondering what your partner is doing whenever you are not with him/her.

If your gut is telling you that something is off, then you should first communicate with your partner about your doubts and insecurities. If he/she refuses to engage with you on this, then, more often than not, there is something else going on that could significantly affect your relationship with them.

Tolerating this kind of relationship can be tiresome, especially since it will lead you to overthink things between the two of you.

- Your partner usually makes big decisions for both of you and without consulting you beforehand.

Re-evaluate your relationship if your partner is the only one calling all the shots. It does not have to be as big as buying a house for both of you without consulting you beforehand. Going to events alone that he/she wants to go to reflects the uneven balance of power between the two of you.

- Sometimes, you need to be alone for a moment, but your partner refuses to give you space.

Self-care is important whether or not you are in a relationship. Wanting some time alone does not mean that you have a problem with your partner. If your partner does not understand that, even after you have explained your reasons to him/her, then your boundaries are being ignored. That is not a good sign because it may develop further into control issues later on.

- You feel responsible for the happiness of your partner.

If your partner relies on you and only you to be happy, then it can cause an imbalance in your mental and emotional state. For example, your partner blames you whenever he/she is upset or angry. Moreover, he/she expects you to remedy the situation or change yourself to make them feel better.

Such a situation can put a lot of strain on you mentally and emotionally. Feeling like you have to walk on eggshells around them, just to keep them happy, is a sign that you are in a toxic relationship.

- Your partner controls or at least try to control what you do and who you spend time with.

  Many relationship experts consider this as the biggest red flag that you should look out for. If your partner wants to control your finances, your relationships with other people, or even your appearance, then you should take a step back from him/her. Take a serious look at your relationship, and communicate your concerns about his/her control issues over you. How they respond to this would determine whether or not the relationship is worth saving.

- You ask yourself if you are in a bad relationship.

  Ignoring the significance of this question can be a source of regret for you later. The simple fact that you are wondering about this is a sign that something is off about your relationship with him/her.

  Rather than overthink the answer to this question, it is best to take a more proactive approach. Talk to your partner and see if things can still be changed for the better. If not, then you should get out of that relationship before you get hurt any further.

Though these signs are mainly for romantic relationships, most of these red flags are also applicable to other types of relationships that you have in your life. For instance, having an overly dependent friend can too be taxing for your wellbeing. A controlling family member can be just as toxic as a controlling partner.

Evaluate all the relationships in your life, and see if any of them are leading you to engage in overthinking, or causing you to feel anxiety. Once you have accepted the fact that there is a problem, then it will be easier for you to find the motivation to move on with your life without them.

Let Go of Certain People

Now that you can identify the relationships that are holding you back, you may now start working on how to let go of them. By doing so, you would also leave more space in your life for positive people who share similar interests, values, and outlook in life as you have.

It is highly likely that you have an idea of what kind of relationships you want to have— about the quality of your friends you want or the characteristics you expect of your significant other. Normally, you would avoid people who bring negativity and distractions along with them. If your goal in life is to be happy and free from your worries, then why would you choose to be with someone who makes you feel anxious?

It may sound obvious to you now, but the fact is, many people fail to let go of these types of people in their life. The insecurities that one possesses, as well as the fear of ending up all alone in life, may prevent common sense from taking over. As a result, bad relationships persist, and so do negative thoughts and feelings that one might have.

Be more selective of your relationships since they usually have more influence over your thoughts and actions than you realize. Surround yourself with people who prefer seeing the brighter things in life, rather than those who like to sulk and mope around. Find someone who shares your dreams, so that you can have a worthy companion while you are on your way to attaining them.

Tips to Shake Off Bad Relationships from Your Life

To help you move on from the relationships you have identified as problematic, here are three important tips that you can apply to get rid of the toxic people in your life finally:

- Set and stick to your boundaries.

    Establish clear guidelines on how you will move on and impose them upon yourself. Even if they try to break through the walls you have put up around yourself, keep them up no matter what.

    If you have told yourself that you will stop all forms of communication with them, then do not respond to their texts and calls. Block them from your phone and social media accounts. Do not be tempted to check in on them because you have decided that you are already done with them.

- Stop being overly accommodating to their needs and wants.

    Toxic people will try to take advantage of whatever fondness and concern that you have for them. Being too nice can be detrimental to your progress in moving on from the relationship.

You do not have to be mean to them, however. Just stop trying to make them feel better about the end of your relationship. You are not responsible for their happiness.

- Be firm with your decision.

   Keep in mind that the decision you have made is based on significant reasons to move on from the relationship. If you have trouble remembering them, write them down in your journal. By doing so, you will be able to remind yourself why you need to be firm with your decision, especially when the person you have removed from your life tries to get back in.

   In the case of toxic family members, it can be hard to break off the relationship completely. For such breakups, the best thing you can do is to impose clear limitations on your future interactions with them.

I would share a personal experience on this subject. I once had a colleague when I was still in the business of the 9-5 work-life, who was more of a friend than a colleague. We would get along happily at work. Then all of a sudden, on one fateful regular workday, her attitude toward me changed. It is like she never knew me or we have never met. I made many attempts to figure out what happened or why she was acting so cold around me and indifferent toward me, but all proved to be unsuccessful. I felt it was unfair to be treated so cold, given our friendly history. The thought of bumping into her during work and getting those negative vibes from her sure gave me cold feet, made me anxious, triggered this worry and overthinking loop of what to do or not to do whenever our paths crossed. I felt her opinion of me mattered, and this was taking a toll on my health, my relationship with other colleagues, and, to some extent, on my work. I quickly realized the negative impact of her attitude toward me on my mental state. Then I decided I had had enough of her shenanigans. No more of such was I taking from her, and no more would she cause me to be anxious and worried.

What did I do?

Your guess is as good as my response.

I decided I was going to ignore her attitude toward me, never caring what she thought of me or her opinions about me, stop any further unwarranted communication with her that isn't work-related, and continued living and working like she never existed — literally speaking. That is not to say I disrespected her in any way when doing any of these, but I was simply numb to her presence around me, and sure, this felt good, and I had a great sense of relief from having to be anxious when we bumped into each other.

The bottom line is, the more time you spend away from the people you are trying to get rid of, the better your chances of completely moving on. The time that will be freed up by your breakup can be spent on doing things for yourself or seeking other people who would infuse more positivity into your life.

Let go of those who bring you misery and welcome those who will bring you happiness.

Let's find out how Amy was able to handle a similar situation like mine with her colleagues.

Case Study

Another source of Amy's anxiety is her work colleagues. She was one of the recent additions to the team, so she still had not yet figured out their personalities and work ethics.

Amy's main problem with some of them is the unsolicited comments about her style of teaching and the way she dressed up for work. Due to her anxiety, she had never communicated with them how she felt upon hearing those comments. She was particularly worried that doing so would only alienate her further from them.

Since she had taken up the initiative to stop engaging in overthinking, Amy mustered up the courage to strike up a conversation with Dorothy, one of the teachers who had been pretty vocal about her opinions of her.

During their conversation, Amy realized that the comments were mostly rooted in the generational gap that existed between the two of them. Before ending the conversation, Amy had asked Dorothy to refrain from making comments about her work and her appearance, especially in front of other teachers and students.

Dorothy promised that she would stop, but after two days, Amy had overheard Dorothy talking about her again. This time, her colleague was complaining about the way Amy had confronted her the other day.

Despite feeling hurt, Amy decided to walk away for now. She needed to cool her head down before forming up a plan to resolve this issue.

N.B: To find out how Amy eventually handled the situation with her colleagues, kindly read through to the last chapter.

Practice Test

Based on the points that you have learned in this chapter, answer the following questions about Amy's problem with some of her colleagues:

- Do you think Amy should have confronted Dorothy about the comments on Amy's teaching style and appearance? Why or why not?

- Does Amy's work relationship with Dorothy show any of the warning signs of a bad relationship? Please specify the red flags that you are seeing in their relationship as colleagues.

- If you were in Amy's shoes, how would you treat Dorothy after the recent incident?

Chapter 7

Pursue Your Goals

"I don't focus on what I'm up against. I focus on my goals, and I try to ignore the rest."

—Venus Williams

Pursuing your goals is most often easier said than done. The thought of having to take that big step to change your career path or quitting your job to start and own your own business, write and publish that long-overdue book or books you keep pushing off all in a bid to pursue your goals can be overwhelming, scary and harder to follow through—not necessarily because they are impossible to accomplish, but because they inherently come with an excessive amount of anxieties, negative thoughts, and worries:

- That a million things could go wrong if you embark on this journey.
- That you "may" fail.

- Of what people will think and so on.

It is one thing to set a goal to discontinue the use of certain social media apps on your phone or the internet and fall flat of it, and it is another thing entirely to pursue your life dream only to realize it has been nothing more of a pipe-dream.

Overcoming the feeling of anxieties, negative thoughts, and worries to go after your goals may not be easy, but it is possible, absolutely possible. And I will show you how you can achieve this and be accountable to it in the subsequent paragraphs. One thing is for sure and certain, pursuing your goals vis-à-vis your passions, are one of the most gratifying and fulfilling feelings you could ever wish for. It automatically gives you a heightened sense of purpose, accomplishment, peace, and happiness. You can take this to the bank.

To get started on pursuing your goals, permit me to hold you by your hand as I take the lead (*laughs*).

Discover Your Vocation

Starting in early childhood, parents, teachers, and maybe even friends have asked you this question: what do you want to be when you grow up? Up to your teenage years, plans in life often tend to be vague yet grand. The pressure usually begins to mount during the latter part, when people are about to choose the degree they will pursue in the university, or when they are trying to start a career out of their gained knowledge, talents, and skills.

Therein lies the problem because many people tend to go with what feels okay at the moment. As a result, they switch majors or jobs within the first few couples of years after they have made a decision.

There is nothing wrong with seeking your passions by trying out different things. However, since most people do not yet have a concrete idea of what they want to achieve in life, their decisions to go for a degree or a job are mostly based on what they are trying to avoid—not what they want to do. For instance, they do not want to be stuck in a mundane 9-to-5 job—something like what their fathers and mothers used to do.

That is a shaky foundation for something that you will be doing for around forty years of your life. Having the answer to what you want to be when you grow up is the ideal basis for this kind of decision. However, if that is too hard for you to answer, even now that you are in your adulthood, then perhaps the question that you should be asking yourself is this: what is your vocation?

If you are familiar with the concept of a vocation, here is how it compares to the other two perspectives that one may have about work:

- Job

    A job is a simple means to an end. By doing your job, you will get a paycheck. That paycheck is needed for your day-to-day expenses, for supporting your family, and for paying rent—which is where most of the paycheck typically goes.

    People with jobs look forward to breaks from their work, especially extended ones where they can take a vacation. Even though their jobs are not horrible or completely mundane, whatever they do for work offers little to no life satisfaction at all.

- Career

    People with careers get their satisfaction not from their work itself, but from the possible advancements that they can make by being good at what they do. They are excited about moving up through the ranks, earning a higher salary, and getting better benefits.

As such, careerists do not find it hard to put in extra time to their day-to-day work. They are eager to move up, so they opt to work as hard as they can. However, when the opportunity to move upward is taken away, or when they have nowhere else to go in the field of work they have chosen, then their satisfaction dives down, thus turning their enthusiasm into frustration and disappointment.

- Vocation

    Your calling or vocation refers to the work you do just for its own sake. You will know it is a vocation when you almost feel like you would still happily do the work even if you do not get paid for it. It would make you think that this is exactly what you are meant to do.

    Though vocations have a reputation for being low-paying work, that only holds true during the start. Once you have established yourself and your passion has translated into the quality of work that you do, then you will receive your due, usually many times over. The money and prestige that you can get by finding and applying your vocation, however, are peripheral only to the ultimate benefit that you can get from it.

Your calling allows you to pursue your passions in life in a gratifying way. The work you do makes you feel that you are contributing to a greater good that goes beyond your personal welfare. Furthermore, applying a vocation allows you to make use of special gifts and talents.

Comparing these three, those who work for a job feels the least happiness and satisfaction in life. This is followed by people with a career, while those who have found and followed their calling tend to be the happiest and most satisfied with what they do.

Such an observation is not surprising because a vocation does not only affect your work life. It reflects your true purpose in life. When you find your calling, you will notice the effects in profound ways. Your life will be filled with joy and fulfilment.

People who have not found their vocation yet often find themselves wondering if what they are doing now is what they would want to be doing for the rest of their lives. A great weight will build up in their chest as time goes by.

Discovering your true calling in life is not something that you would usually stumble upon. You may be doing a job that utilizes your talent, but it does fulfil you because the purpose is not related to your passion. You may also be working in a field close to your passions, but the employer does not allow you to make significant contributions using your talent. Neither of these scenarios is ideal for your pursuit of fulfilment from your work.

Therefore, to find your true vocation, you need to recognize not only your skills and talents but also your passions in life.

What Motivates You? – Your Passions

Discovering your passion is not as hard as you think it is. The answer, however, is critical in determining what you want to do in life. This is not limited to those who are just about to enter the university or the workforce. It is also a common problem among those who feel bored, lost, or unfulfilled with their current jobs.

To figure out what truly motivates you, here are some suggestions that you can try out for yourself.

- Answer these three questions.
    - Which topic can you read a thousand books about without getting bored out of your mind?
    - What is the one thing that you do not mind doing for a whole decade without getting paid?
    - How would you spend your time if you are so financially secure that you do not have to work for a living?

    If your answers to these questions have a common theme at the very least, then that is likely your passion in life.

- Visualize your dream job.

    Imagine yourself waking up in the morning even before your alarm has gone off. You dress up quickly, not because you are running late but because you are excited to go to work. The sun is shining brightly outside, and you take a step outside your home. Where are you heading to? What are you about to do when you get to work?

Your passions may be found with the help of your subconscious mind. Let your imagination run free to discover what lies beneath your doubt, worries, and insecurities.

- Recall what you loved doing when you were just a kid.

Did you enjoy drawing pictures or baking cookies with your mom? Do you want to continue doing that now that you are an adult? What are your hobbies that started when you were young and persists to be an interest up to this day? Make these memories as your reference on what you would want to do now.

- Ask your family and close friends for advice.

You do not have to shoulder everything when trying to discover your passions in life. The people who know you best might have some important inputs that can lead you to the right answer.

Do not put them on the spot, however. Let them think about it for some time. This will ensure that what you are getting from them is something worthy of serious consideration.

Note Down Your Life Goals

Now that you have a better idea of what you want to achieve, it is best to write them down in your journal. According to experts, tangibly recording them improves one's odds in transforming them into reality.

The simple act of documenting your goals prompts the subconscious mind to begin thinking of them as opportunities. This is not possible if you are merely thinking of your goals because the brain handles so many things all at once that your goals might be completely overlooked and forgotten.

To start building a habit of noting down your life goals, here is an exercise that you should try doing every morning for the following seven days. In a journal, write down your goals for each important aspect of your life. You can add it to the list below.

- Personal health
- Relationships
- Vocation

Go beyond what you think you can have, or what seems possible at this moment in your life. Instead, write down goals that you want to achieve, regardless of how grand or ambitious it may sound to you right now.

Though this exercise may seem simple, it will enable you to:

- Achieve a higher clarity about your life goals; and
- Recognize the value of opportunities that come your way based on how they would help you achieve your goals.

It is not enough, however, to simply know what you want to do. You also need to gain and sustain the drive to pursue them relentlessly, despite the challenges, anxieties, and worries that you might face along the way. This is how your passions in life can enhance your strategies to achieve your goals.

Connect Goals to Passions and Prioritize Them

You need to make time for your passions since they will lead you to your true purpose in life. To do so, you need to focus on them by centering your goals around your passions in life.

Since you are motivated to pursue what you love, then you would also be more driven to push past the challenges and achieve your goals.

In an ideal world, you will attain whatever you have set your mind to achieve. However, in reality, you can only do so much at a time, no matter how motivated you are. You must, therefore, learn how to prioritize the important life goals that you have on your list.

To do so, here are some guide questions that can help you set your priorities. Answer them truthfully to come up with a list of passion-driven goals that you need to prioritize. It is best to write down your answers in your journal so that you can reflect on them after answering these questions.

- Which of your goals do you think of the most?
- Which of your goals would energize you the most once you have committed to them?

- Which goal would make you feel the proudest once you have accomplished it?

- Which goal would have personal importance to you for the rest of your life?

- Which of your goals is completely aligned with your values?

- Which of your goals is within the bounds of your control and not entirely dependent on your current circumstance or some other person?

Since you have written down your responses, you can review them to gain insight into what your priorities should be. Do not force yourself, though. Take your time. You may even re-do the questions if you are not satisfied with what you can glean off of them.

Once you have assigned priorities to your goals, then you are now ready to proceed in making them more manageable.

Set S.M.A.R.T. Goals

This refers to a goal-setting strategy that translates vaguely written goals into more defined and actionable items. Through this, you would be able to clarify what you should be doing, when you should accomplish it, and how you would know if you have successfully attained them.

The acronym S.M.A.R.T. stands for:

- Specific

    Your goal should be clearly stated so that you would know exactly what you are trying to achieve.

- Measurable

    Through this, you will be able to monitor your progress and stay focused on meeting your projected timeline. As you draw closer to your goal, you would also feel more motivated to push through until the end of the line.

- Achievable

    A goal has to be based on your reality so that you may have a chance to achieve it. However, do not set your goal so low because it will negatively affect your motivation and sense of fulfillment. The sweet spot is somewhere a bit further than your comfort zone. It should stretch you a bit, but not too much that it may strain you.

- Relevant

    This would ensure that the goal you are pursuing is significant to you. Otherwise, you might lose your drive eventually, thus wasting whatever time, effort, and resources that you have already exerted to achieve the said goal.

- Time-Bound

    A goal needs a due date to be effective. Otherwise, you would not be able to impose your priorities well.

How to Set S.M.A.R.T. Goals that WORKS!

To help you effectively apply the principles of S.M.A.R.T. to your goals, here are some essential questions you should answer.

- Specific

    You may define your goal in great detail by answering the 5 "W" questions:

    - What do you want to achieve?

    - Why is this goal significant to you?

- Who are the people involved in achieving this goal?
- Where is it going to take place?
- Which of your resources and limitations would apply to this goal?

- **Measurable**

    You may assess the measurability of your goal if it addresses the following questions:

    - How many/much _____ do you need to achieve your goal?
    - How will you know if you have already achieved your goal?

- **Achievable**

    To make your goal attainable, answer the following guide questions:

    - What strategy/strategies are you going to use to accomplish your goal?
    - How realistic is your goal against your current personal limitations (i.e., skills, talents, financial status, etc.)?

- Relevant

    A goal is relevant to you if you can answer "yes" to the following questions:

    - Is the goal worth your time, effort, and resources?
    - Is it the right time to pursue this goal?
    - Is it aligned with your other goals and needs in life?

- Time-Bound

    You can establish the timeline for your goal by answering these questions:

    - When do you need to accomplish this goal?
    - What can you do today/___ week from now/___ month from now/___ year from now to get closer to your goal?

To make your S.M.A.R.T. goals even more effective, you should positively construct them. For example, rather than saying, "Do not skip breakfast," you should say, "Eat a healthy and balanced meal during breakfast time every day."

You should also reflect upon your list of S.M.A.R.T. goals regularly. Set a schedule for your reviews and personal evaluations. This will help you keep your list up-to-date vis-à-vis your current situation and what you have achieved so far.

If you have diligently followed through with this very chapter, I believe you should have been able to gain an enormous amount of inner strength and insights that have not only helped you to discover your vocation (if you haven't before now) but to also help you in pursuing your goals to the finish line without having to feel any form of anxiety, negative thought or worry of not pulling through.

Case Study

Aside from making to-do lists, Amy had also decided to set effective goals that will ultimately lead her to stop overthinking on how to go about pursuing and achieving her goals. To do this, she applied the principles of S.M.A.R.T. goals.

Using her list of recurring triggers as her basis, Amy formed goals for the successful resolution of each trigger. For example, under the trigger prompted by her upcoming performance appraisal, she wrote down this goal:

"At least one week before the performance appraisal, conduct a dry run of the proposed lesson plan to be used for the evaluation with a different set of students."

Practice Test

Analyze Amy's sub-goal to ace the performance appraisal vis-à-vis the elements of S.M.A.R.T. goal-setting strategy. Evaluate how well Amy had implemented these principles of this strategy. Indicate the good points and the points for improvement for each element. You may use the guide questions above as a point of reference in your evaluation when setting your goals.

- Specific?

    _____
    _____
    _____
    _____

- Measurable?

_____
_____
_____
_____

- Achievable?

_____
_____
_____
_____

- Realistic?

_____
_____
_____
_____

- Time-Bound?

_____
_____
_____
_____

Chapter 8

Practice Mindfulness

"Remember then: there is only one important time—now! It is the most important time because it is the only time when we have any power."

—Leo Tolstoy

What is Mindfulness?

When your mind is fully focused on what is currently happening to you, on what you are doing, and on the environment where you live in, you are experiencing the phenomenon called mindfulness.

It might seem like something that anyone can do naturally. After all, everyone possesses the potential to achieve this quality through practice.

However, the human mind is prone to wandering. At that point, you will lose touch with what your body is feeling and going through. If this goes on further, obsessive and intrusive thoughts will begin invading your mind, filling it with negative thoughts and worries about the future. In time, this can lead to full, blown anxiety.

Fortunately, no matter how far your mind has gone, mindfulness can bring you back to the present, where you can be, once again, completely aware of your actions and feelings.

Why You Need to Practice Mindfulness

Practicing mindfulness allows you to have better access to its benefits. According to experts, mindfulness can:

- Reduce your level of stress;
- Enable you to gain insight about your inner self;
- Improve your self-awareness, particularly about your thoughts;
- Enhance your physical and mental performance;
- Make you feel happier;
- Increase your level of patience;
- Make you more accepting of the changes in your life; and

- Lower down your feelings of frustration and disappointment.

Mindfulness also fosters your ability to see things from the perspective of others. Through this, you may be able to relieve yourself of your negative thoughts and worries about how others think or feel about you.

For example, your friend snapped at you when you had asked her about her day. At first, you might worry about whether or not you have done something to upset her.

However, if you could set aside this automatic response for even a moment, then you might be able to recall that she mentioned something about having a hard time finishing up a paper. You could then surmise that her foul mood may have resulted from being stressed out by her deadline.

This alternative explanation of your friend's behavior may help alleviate your earlier worries about your actions towards her. You would also feel less bad about being unintentionally snapped at by your friend.

Effective Techniques for Practicing Mindfulness

Even though mindfulness is an innate human ability, you can still improve your access to it by applying various techniques, such as:

- Mindful Meditation

    This technique works best if you would do it in a quiet spot that is free from clutter. It should be well ventilated and well lighted, ideally by natural light.

    Once you have found the perfect spot for this, you must follow these steps to perform mindful meditation properly:

    o Take a seat.

        It can be a chair, a bench, or a floor cushion, as long as it is stable and comfortable.

    o Adjust the position of your legs.

        If you are sitting on a chair or a bench, it is best to keep both feet on the ground. If you are sitting down on the floor, then you should cross both your legs in front of you.

o Adopt a straight posture for your upper body.

Do not overdo it by straining your spine out of its natural curvature. The angle of your head and shoulders must feel comfortable to prevent their positions from being a source of distraction for you later on.

o Place your upper arms in a parallel position to your upper body.

o Gently place your hands on top of your legs.

Maintain the positioning of your upper arms from the previous step. This will keep you from either slouching forward or leaning too far back.

o Slowly drop your gaze along with your chin.

You may also lower your upper lid, or even close them if it would make you feel more comfortable. Take note, however, that this is not necessary for mindful meditation.

- Relax, and be there at the moment.

  Observe if you would feel any unusual sensations in your body.

- Feel and follow your breathing.

  Take note of the air flowing in through your nose or mouth. Observe how your chest or stomach rise and fall with each breath you take.

- When other thoughts enter your mind, do not block them.

  Instead, just gently realign your focus on your breathing once you have noticed that you have drifted away.

- If you need to move your body, take a quick pause before acting upon it.

  There are times when you have to move a body part to feel more comfortable. Sometimes, you would also feel an itch that you just have to scratch. You are allowed to move your body as long as the movement is deliberate and intentional on your part. The pause that you will take before each movement would enable you to make this transition a success.

- When you feel relaxed yet focused, you may lift your gaze and chin once more.

If you had closed your eyes, then you may now open them. Once you do, take note of how your body feels during that moment. Notice the first thoughts and emotions that will rise to the surface as well.

Based on what you have noted, decide on how you should proceed with the rest of your day.

In case you want to incorporate music into your mindful meditation session, then you can try using the iOS and Android app called "Relax Melodies." Unlike most other meditation apps that include guided meditation tracks, this one only contains background music that you can use while meditating. Therefore, this is an excellent option for those who already have experience in mindful meditation but want to enhance their experience further. Since this app is for free, feel free to try it and see if it would be of any use to you.

- Mindful Observation

    Through this exercise, you will be able to gain a better and deeper appreciation of even the simplest elements in your current environment. Thus, you will feel a connection with the natural beauty of the things around you—something that would not have been possible because you always seem to be in a rush to go somewhere else.

    To do this, you must:

    - Choose a natural object that can be found within your field of sight.

        This can be a plant, the clouds in the sky, or even an insect.

    - Focus and observe it for a minute or two.

        Do not engage in anything else while you are doing this. Try to relax your body and mind as you do so.

- Look at the object with awe and wonderment, as if this is the first time that you see it.

- Explore with your eyes the form of the object.

    Let your attention be consumed by its mere presence.

- Allow yourself to connect with the object in terms of its role in the natural world, and based on the general vibes that you are getting from it.

* Mindful Listening

This technique involves the presence of two elements: attention and intention. If you can stay in the present, and remain open and unbiased no matter what you hear, then you have the element of focus.

On the other hand, the element of intention is present when you possess a genuine interest in what the other person is saying.

Mindful listening, however, is not simply listening well to others. It also pertains to an individual's ability to listen well to himself/herself. If you are not aware of your personal beliefs, needs, aspirations, and fears, then you will not have much capacity to listen to somebody else's.

To help you apply this technique, here are some essential tips about mindful listening:

- Check inward first.

    If you are feeling something off or unpleasant, then you have to address that first before engaging with others.

- Get a feel of your own presence.

    Let the other person feel your interest and feelings of empathy, too.

- Take note in the silence of any reactions you might have.

    Quickly note your reactions as they arise, and then return your attention to the speaker.

- Make the other person feel heard.

You may do this by reflecting upon the speaker's words and saying back a summary of his/her main points.

- o Keep things going by using open-ended questions.

    You may ask questions to clarify points that you do not understand and to probe for more information.

- Mindful Breathing

    You may practice this in whatever position is most comfortable for you. Keeping your eyes open or closed also depends on which one would make you concentrate more.

    As a guide, here is a short step-by-step process on how to do mindful breathing:

    - o Assume a comfortable position that will relax your body.
    - o Pay attention to the shape of your body and the sensations that you can feel across different body parts.
    - o Switch your focus to your breathing.

- Feel the natural flow of air in and out of your body.
- Take note of the sensations in between each breath.
- If your mind starts drifting off to other topics while doing this exercise, acknowledge first that you are straying off from the path by whispering under your breath "wondering" or "thinking." Then, gently realign your focus back to your breathing.
- After around 5 minutes, switch your attention back to the rest of your body.
- Feel how more relaxed you are now.
- Proceed with the rest of your day more mindfully.

- Mindful Walking

This technique is particularly useful because you will walk at some point during the day. You can better utilize that time spent walking by engaging your body and mind with a mindful and meditative exercise.

To guide you through this here is one form of mindful walking that you can do even while walking down a street:

- Assume a straight posture.
- Curl in the thumb of your left hand, and then close the rest of your fingers over it.
- Place your left hand in the spot above your belly button.
- Place your right hand over your left hand, resting the right thumb in the space between the left thumb and the left index finger.
- Slightly drop your gaze.
- Take your first step using your left foot.
- Take another step using your right foot.
- Follow a steady, mindful pace.
- If your mind wanders off, bring it back by focusing again on the sensations of your feet as they touch the ground.

- Guided Meditation

If you do not know where and how to start meditating properly, you may consider trying guided meditations. Through this, you will be able to practice conjuring up mental imageries as you meditate or incorporate different breathing exercises into your routine. Others also teach you how to create personal mantras that you can use for meditation.

There are various sources of guided meditations, including:

- Apps

    Go through the app store on your phone or tablet to find one that would suit your needs. Take note, however, that the popularity of the app does not indicate its quality. Read through the description, and if possible, reviews from actual users to get a better sense of what you may expect from the app.

    Here are some of the suggested apps geared for beginners:

    a. "Mindfulness Training"

You can get the first two lessons for free in the iOS app store. From these two lessons, you will be able to get 6 sample guided meditations that you can try out for yourself.

b. "Headspace"

This app may be downloaded for both iOS and Android devices. Its main purpose is to be your personal trainer when it comes to your daily meditation practice. You can get this out for free for the first ten days. After that, you will have the option to proceed by subscribing to it for a month, a year, or even a lifetime.

c. "Simply Being"

Through this app, you may be able to customize your meditation experience. You can set your preferred duration for each session, as well as the sounds that you can hear to make the session more immersive. You may choose from nature sounds, guiding voices, music, or a combination of any of these three. This is available on the iOS and Android platforms for $1.99.

- Podcasts

There are various podcasts available nowadays on the topic of meditation, as well as quick guided meditation practices that you can use to learn the ropes in your own time. Here a few suggested podcasts you can try out based on their popularity. A simple search of these on Google would direct you to where you can listen to these podcasts.

   a. The daily meditation podcast with Mary Meckley

   b. 10% happier with Dan Harris

   c. Tara Brach

   d. The meditation Oasis

   e. Meditation Minis

- Reflect on Your Thoughts

The objective of this mindfulness exercise is to establish a deeper connection with your thoughts. Here are some tips that you can do to practice this:

  - You can start this by asking yourself first about the things that you are grateful for.
  - To prevent the logical part of your brain from answering, experts suggest referring to yourself in the second person.

    As such, the correct form of a possible starting question is, "What are you feeling most grateful for right now?"

  - Thoughts related to this question would surely come to the forefront of your mind.
  - Stay connected to the natural flow of your thoughts.

    Avoid trying to direct it in a different direction.

○ Form a deep connection with your thoughts as you continue paying your complete attention to them.

To keep yourself from being immersed in this activity for too long, you may use an app, such as the "Insight Timer," to preset a duration for each session. The benefit of using apps like this is that its method of notifying you is significantly less jarring than the alarm timer on your phone. As a result, you will be able to retain the mindful state that you have entered, even after the session has ended.

- Self-Compassion Break

    This technique serves as a personal reminder to apply mindfulness, kindness, and common humanity—the three core components of self-compassion—whenever you are facing difficulties in your life.

    For this method to be effective, you have to make use of the soothing properties of human touch. You must also find a way to communicate with yourself effectively. It will only distract you if you cannot agree with yourself about the meaning of your words.

Here is a step-by-step process on how to conduct a self-compassion break. Ideally, you should be doing this with your eyes closed to focus more on your inner self.

- o Think of a personal life situation that is making you feel stressed out.

  This may be a health issue, problems with your partner or family member, financial difficulties, or work struggles.

- o Select a specific problem within that aspect.

  It should not be that big of a problem. You have just started doing this, so it is best to stick to the mild to moderate range for now.

- o Visualize your chosen situation.

  Picture in your mind the setting of the situation. If there is dialogue involved, identify the speakers and who is saying what to whom. Go into the details of what is happening and what might happen.

- Take note of the sensations in your body.

  Are you feeling any sort of discomfort while you are visualizing the situation in your mind? If you do not, then you should go back to step 2 and choose a slightly more stressful problem.

- When you feel discomfort in your body, recognize it for what it is.

  You may try saying the following statements, whichever sounds right to you. By doing this, you are exhibiting mindfulness.

    a. "This is a moment of suffering."

    b. "This moment is painful for me."

    c. "This is so stressful."

- To channel your common humanity, acknowledge that struggle is part of the normal human experience.

  You may do so by saying out loud any of these statements:

    a. "Suffering is a part of being human."

b. "I am not alone. Everyone suffers at some point in their lives."

c. "Other people feel this kind of pain, too when they are struggling."

o Offer yourself a gesture that would soothe yourself, along with a message of kindness to yourself.

This may be expressed through the following sample statements:

a. "May I accept myself as I am."

b. "May I be kind to myself."

c. "May I be patient. May I be strong."

d. "May I provide for myself whatever I need."

If you cannot think of the right words to say to yourself, then imagine offering support to a family member or a close friend who is suffering from a similar problem as you. What are the words that you will choose then? How can you deliver your message of kindness to those you care about?

Think about this, and see if you can offer the same kind of treatment and support to yourself.

- Body Scan

  Through similar principles of meditation, this technique can enable you to establish a deep connection with your body. As the name implies, it involves a conscious scanning of your body, from the top of your head to the tip of your toes.

  During the process, you will become hyper-aware of any unusual sensations, discomfort, and pains within your body. These are crucial pieces of information because, depending on their location, these may be indicators of an anxious mind and a worn-out body.

  To apply this technique, allocate at least 30 minutes for this activity. It is also best to lie down on a mat or a bed, but you may also do this in a sitting position. Choose whichever position would allow you to stay awake and alert throughout the following activity.

    o Close your eyes.

This will help you keep your focus on what matters. If you are not comfortable with this, you may just half-close your eyes.

- Take note of your breathing and your point of contact with the surface you are lying on or sitting on.

Take as much time as you need to examine the movement and specified areas of your body.

- Once you are ready, take a deep breath before moving on to the examination of another body part.

You can either follow a system wherein you examine everything from your head down to your toes, or you may choose which areas to observe randomly.

- Take note of any sensation you are currently feeling in the body part you are examining.

These sensations include, but are not limited to, tightness, tingling, high or low temperature, pressure, or buzzing. If you cannot feel anything, then that is perfectly fine. Take note of that too.

Your objective for this step is to simply notice your current feelings and sensations. Do not judge anything yet at this point.

- After you have explored the sensations from different parts of your body, expand the scope of your attention to your whole body.

    Spend a few minutes just breathing in and out freely as you get an overall feel of your bodily sensations.

- You may now proceed with the rest of your day.

    Make your movements more deliberate than usual to retain your current mental state for a longer period.

Case Study

Another strategy that Amy had taken up was practicing mindfulness. Since she was a beginner, she selected guided meditations as her preferred method. She downloaded an app on her phone and set a schedule for her session.

Though she found it hard to achieve a mindful state during her first try, she did notice that she felt more relaxed and calmer after the activity. Because of this, she decided to include this in her weekly to-do list.

Practice Test

Download at least one of the suggested apps for guided meditation given earlier in this chapter. Just like Amy, try out a session, and then answer the following questions based on your experience:

- How do you feel after doing this activity?
- Do you think you have met your goal for this activity? Why or why not?
- Would you try doing this again until it becomes one of your habits? Why or why not?

Chapter 9

Be Happy

If we would just slow down, happiness would catch up to us.

— Richard Carlson

As confirmed by multiple studies, happiness is crucial to one's overall mental health. Happy people tend to have better relationships with the people around them. They find it easier to pursue their true passions in life, and therefore find success in what they have chosen to do. Their happiness also protects them from harmful elements that could lower down the quality of their life, such as overthinking and anxiety.

Attaining happiness in your life is not an easy feat to achieve. Some people assume that there are special techniques that will make them happy overnight. However, that is what makes happiness elusive to them.

Rather than a destination that you need to go to, happiness is found in the journey itself. It is a way of life that makes you feel fulfilled and contented. No matter what your status in life is, you can find happiness with the people around you and in the things that you do.

Live Your Best Life: There Is Only One to Live

You need to make the most out of the life you currently have by finding happiness, purpose, and satisfaction in your life.

A lot of people tend to forget that they have a choice on how to live their lives. They let themselves be stuck in their miserable situations, complaining and whining about how unfair everything is around them.

It is natural for humans to dream for the best possible future for them. However, this can only go so far if that is the only thing that you will do. You have to take action and live your life in the best possible way. This goes beyond simple wishful thinking. It involves finding your true purpose in life and pursuing your passions.

Living up to your full potential is only one way to go about this, though. You can also aim to live a well-balanced life. By figuring out the right balance in the key areas of your life, you would be able to go after the things that will make you happy and fulfilled.

To live your best life, you must commit to creating this kind of life for yourself. You have to commit to facing the challenges of personal growth and development. Only then can you have the strength, courage, and determination to live your best life.

Steps You Can Take to Be Happy

You are in charge of finding your happiness. To guide you through this, here are some actionable steps that you can take right now:

- Add more foods that are rich in tyrosine into your diet.

  Tyrosine is an amino acid that increases the production of dopamine—or also known as the feel-good hormone—in your brain. Excellent sources of tyrosine include almonds, avocados, bananas, and eggs.

- Practice relaxation exercises regularly.

  You may go for a nice massage or a long walk in the park. Meditation has also been proven to be an effective way of calming both the body and the mind.

- Get enough high-quality sleep.

This means that upon waking up, you feel well-rested and more energized. To achieve this, some people set a regular sleeping schedule that enables the REM cycle to complete its course. Others design a sleeping ritual that would put the body and mind into the optimal sleeping condition.

- Make your fitness a priority.

Exercising regularly increases the dopamine levels in your brain. You do not have to get a gym subscription for this to be effective. You can go for simple activities such as power walking, running, lifting weights, or swimming.

- Practice mindfulness.

Pay complete attention to everything you do. Avoid giving in to distractions and immerse yourself with the moment. You can practice this by adopting any of your preferred mindfulness techniques elucidated in the previous chapter.

- Be grateful

    Keep track of the things that you feel thankful for.

    This may be the people you cherish in your life, or the places you frequent to, or the work projects that you are currently enjoying. For better results, record them in a journal. By doing so, you will be able to refer to them as well whenever you need a little boost.

- Stop comparing yourself with others.

    There is no point comparing yourself with other people because everyone is likely at different phases in their lives. Comparing yourself against someone who is more established in life would only make you miserable.

- Work for meaningful goals, not money.

    You will be more fulfilled if your work is aligned with your purpose in life. No matter how demanding it is, or how little you get paid for doing it, pursuing your vocation would significantly increase your chances of finding happiness.

- Spend more time with positive people.

One of the basic human needs is socializing. However, it is not just simply the amount of time you spend but also the quality of the time you spend with them. This means that you have to engage in constructive and uplifting activities to generate happiness within you.

The personalities and interests of the people you associate with also factors into your happiness. Ideally, you should select positive-thinking individuals who share similar values as you do.

- Keep good memories, and let go of the bad ones.

   Your memories are your constant companions. Therefore, they can influence your mood and outlook in life in significant ways. Cherish the good memories you have so that you will have a source of inspiration and motivation, especially in times of need.

   Letting go of the negative ones would free you from the burden of having to carry them with you every day. It would also give you more opportunities to appreciate your life in general.

Case Study

Though Amy had begun keeping a list of her blessings, she felt like she was not taking a proactive approach to her happiness. At this point, she was only waiting until something good had happened to her.

To live her best life, Amy started forming a happiness plan. Using her knowledge about effective task management and goal setting, she identified the various ways she can seek out happiness in everything she did.

Feeling more satisfied with this approach, Amy set out to implement her plan to be happier not just at work but in all important areas of her life.

Practice Test

Create your happiness plan using the following table format. You may choose only one area in your life to focus on this exercise. However, feel free to explore all the ways you can think of, as long as you would follow through with the prescribed format.

Area	Goal	Action Plan (To-Do List)
		1.
		2.

3.
1.
2.
3.
1.
2.
3.

Once you have created your plan, answer the following questions:

- Why did you choose these particular areas (s) in your life to be included in the happiness plan?

- Evaluate your happiness goal vis-à-vis the S.M.A.R.T. goal criteria:
    - Specific?
    _____
    _____
    _____

- Measureable?

   _____
   _____
   _____

- Achievable?

   _____
   _____
   _____

- Realistic?

   _____
   _____
   _____

- Time-Bound?

   _____
   _____
   _____

- Based on how well you have made your goals, how do you feel about the happiness action plan that you have made?

A Short message from the Author:

Hey, I hope you are enjoying the book? I would love to hear your thoughts!

Many readers do not know how hard reviews are to come by and how much they help an author.

I would be incredibly grateful if you could take just 60 seconds to write a short review on the product page of this book, even if it is a few sentences!

Thanks for the time taken to share your thoughts!

Your review will genuinely make a difference for me and help gain exposure for my work.

Your review will genuinely make a difference for me and help gain exposure for my work.

Chapter 10

Reach Out to Someone

People suffering from anxiety find it hard to seek out for help due to various reasons. Their tendency to overthink keeps them from acting upon their need for help. They also become more bound to the stigmas associated with mental health issues.

Moreover, the negative thoughts may prevent them from voicing out their concerns out of fear and paranoia, both of which are typically rooted in stigmas and the kind of mental conditioning they have had in their life. This would then translate to worries about being rejected by the people around them and being isolated from those they care about.

In case you are one of these people, know that there are plenty of ways to ask for help. The most accessible one is through the support of your family and friends. However, if you are not comfortable with that, then affordable—sometimes free—therapies conducted with the guidance of a mental health expert are also available nowadays. There are even methods now that allow people to speak out anonymously.

To help you better identify the many ways you can reach out to someone about your mental health issues, the following sections cover the important things you need to keep in mind, especially during challenging times.

Don't be Afraid to Ask for Help

Getting over your fear and worries about reaching out to others is a crucial step in stopping yourself from engaging in overthinking and feeling anxious. As mentioned earlier, the most accessible group of people that you can connect with are those who love you and care about your wellbeing.

To guide you through this, here are the steps you need to take to start effectively communicating with them about this sensitive topic.

- Identify the members of your family and friends that you can trust.

- Schedule a private chat with them on a date and time that is convenient for both of you.

- Open up an honest conversation by admitting that you need help in overcoming your tendency to overthink, your feelings of anxiety, your negative thoughts, and your worries.

- Describe in detail how these mental issues are affecting you in terms of the important aspects of your life, such as your relationships, vocation, and health.

- Be specific about what you need from them so that they can offer you better support.

- Share your safety plan with them so that they will know what to do in case you suffer from panic attacks or any other severe side-effects.

- Promise to keep them up to date about your goal to overcome these issues.

If you are not ready to lay all of these out to the people who know you personally, then you may try joining support groups that are composed of other people who are suffering from similar issues.

In these groups, confidentiality is of the utmost importance to make every member feel safe whenever they open up about their personal experiences. It takes a different kind of courage to admit to strangers the troubles and mistakes in your life. However, the following benefits of doing so typically outweigh these reservations.

- You will likely feel less judged and more understood.

- You are actively encouraged to be open and honest about your thoughts and feelings, no matter how dark and depressing they are.

- The other members are going to share practical tips that have worked for them, and thus may work for you.

- You will get access to relevant resources, such as self-help books and therapists, that can help you resolve your issues.

- After some time, you might feel less lonely and isolated.

Take note that it may take you a while before you can find a support group that will match your needs and preferences. Fortunately, there are plenty of ways to find one that might be compatible with you. You may search online for existing support groups near you, or you may try checking local mental health centers for recommendations. If you are comfortable asking your trusted family members and friends about this, then you may also ask for their advice.

Talk to a Physician If Everything Else Fails

If talking to your loved ones and support groups do not cause any significant improvements, then seriously consider seeking the help of mental health professional.

There are various types of physicians and therapists that you can look for. Each one has its own specialty, but most people who suffer from overthinking and anxiety are advised to get help from those with a background in cognitive-behavioral therapy. This branch of psychology is considered by many as one of the more effective approaches to mental health issues.

Much like support groups, it can be challenging to find a therapist that is compatible with you. You can start finding one through the same methods you have employed in searching for support groups.

Some therapists offer phone consultations so that you can try their services out first before committing to a series of therapy sessions. In case you are not comfortable speaking on the phone with a relative stranger, then an email consultation with a therapist is also pretty common nowadays.

Case Study

Amy has still not resolved her issues with her colleagues at this point. Since her first plan did not work as intended, she sought the help of her best friend, Danny.

After confiding in him about her experiences at work, Amy was surprised to find out that Danny had faced similar challenges when he was just starting at the architectural firm he is working at.

Although different settings, Danny shared with Amy some tips on how he had handled the situation back then. He had also reminded her that she did not have to please everybody and that their opinions would only matter if she would let them get to her.

Feeling well supported and understood, Amy felt more confident that she could get through this issue as well as Danny had done. If not, she knew that he would always have her back.

Practice Test

Answer the following questions about this interaction between Amy and Danny:

- Was Amy right about confiding her work problems to her best friend, Danny? Why or why not?

- Are Danny's pieces of advice actionable for Amy? How do you think Amy would translate Danny's advice into her goals and to-do list?

- Based on all that you have learned so far from this book, what advice would you give to Amy, aside from the ones given already by Danny?

Conclusion

"No one saves us but ourselves. No one can, and no one may. We ourselves must walk the path."

– Buddha

I'd like to thank you and congratulate you for transiting my lines from start to finish.

I hope this book was able to help you understand the causes and effects of overthinking, anxiety, negative thoughts, and worrying in different aspects of your life. I also hope that you were able to find a useful technique that can help you overcome them once and for all.

At this point, you are now better equipped to take control of your thoughts and emotions. In this book, you have learned how to:

- Accept the past, live in the present, and plan better for the future;

- Follow through on your tasks and plans up to completion;

- Optimize your home, relationships, work-life, digital space, and health;

- Set significant and achievable goals in your life; and

- Be more open and honest about your thoughts and feeling to the people who are willing to help you through this.

The next step is to maintain your personal journal as you apply your preferred techniques that have been discussed in the previous chapters of this book. You are free to experiment with which of these strategies would work best with your needs and current situation.

Finally, I want you to take responsibility for your personal wellbeing. Take charge of finding a way to stop overthinking and overcome your anxieties, negative thoughts, and worries by following through with any applicable techniques discussed in the previous chapters. Since you know yourself best—your strengths, limitations, and fears—you know better than anyone which techniques would get you closer to a future that is free from paralyzing thoughts and negative vibes.

Remember, "Knowing is not enough; we must apply. Willing is not enough; we must do", a quote by Goethe.

I wish you the very best!

PART II

Cognitive Behavioral Therapy Made Simple

Effective Strategies to Rewire Your Brain and Instantly Overcome Depression, End Anxiety, Manage Anger, and Stop Panic Attacks in its Tracks.

Introduction

We've all found ourselves being overcome by the firm grip of overwhelming emotions at some point. This could be a feeling of depression that paints life with a gloomy color, dreadful anxiety, excessive anger, panic attacks that strike without warning, or perhaps, other feelings that forcefully overtakes our hearts and minds. When we are emotionally thrown off balance by these feelings, it becomes paramount that we take conscious and intentional steps toward regaining strength to find relief as soon as possible – preventing any further wreckage being done to our overall mental health and wellbeing. During the late stages of my emotional breakdown episode and in my quest for emotional freedom, I came across a unique but fascinating treatment option that seemed quite different from other types of treatments for people who suffered from depression, anxiety, and panic attacks. This treatment option is called cognitive behavioral therapy (CBT). The more I dug deeper into this therapy and its inner workings, the more I realized how depression, anxiety, anger and panic overtake our thoughts, plunging it into harmful directions, and how CBT can help to retrain our thoughts in serving us better. I also learned that when we build more activities into our daily lives that are not only rewarding but fun, they tend to have very powerful antidepressant effects. 'Being present' with positive curiosity and openness, I discovered, is one of the most powerful ways you can break free from anxiety and depression. This approach, the mindfulness-based method, has received wide acceptance and is backed by sufficient research as the "third wave" of CBT, including other cognitive and behavioral techniques.

I have observed that when we are fighting the battle to win back our emotional and mental wellbeing, we usually lack the time, willingness, and energy to go through pages of research findings to find what can work for the given situation. We need straight to the point treatment options that can be used right away. However the case, they are not easy to follow through with as I have learned that even while these treatment options are effective and simple to apply, they do require an amount of work and effort. This is particularly hard to do when you are depressed and demotivated, or when you are fighting back panic attacks. This is where the power of CBT comes into play, providing you with a goal to work toward, as well as carefully designed step by step techniques to help you get there.

As much as possible, I have strived to ensure that the succeeding chapters of this book are simplistic, engaging, and helpful to enable you to overcome your current emotional dilemma. Also, this book has been designed to serve those who haven't heard of CBT, those who currently work with a therapist, or who have made use of CBT in the past but need a new resource as a refresher for up to date information.

At the end of this book, you will;

- Have a better understanding of what CBT means.
- **Understand how your thoughts determine your feelings and behaviors.**
- Discover science-backed research why CBT is a very effective therapeutic option in the treatment of depression, anxiety, anger, and panic attacks.
- Be more aware of what you must do to ensure you get the most out of CBT.
- Be enlightened on how the negative thoughts that fuel your negative emotions develop, and how you can identify them when they come to mind.
- Uncover life hacks that you can apply right away to challenge and replace your negative thoughts with more balanced, healthy, and rational thoughts.
- Know how to make your new, restructured thoughts your second nature, and how to monitor your feelings to prevent a relapse.

- Discover tailored and proven techniques you can start right now and how you can apply them to overcome depression, end anxiety, manage anger, and stop panic attacks in its tracks.
- Begin your journey toward reclaiming your overall health and mental wellbeing with the aid of the carefully structured case studies and practice exercises to guide you along the way.

...and much more!

In conclusion, I am very thrilled to not only share my personal story and struggle with depression, anxiety, and anger but most importantly, I am excited to provide you with a simplistic but yet detailed guide that will truly make your understanding of CBT worthwhile. I hope you find this book really helpful so that nothing gets in your way of living the life you enjoy and love.

Charles's Story

I was moved to write this book, which is my latest work due to my personal experience on the subject and how much so I got fascinated about Cognitive Behavioral Therapy (CBT), especially as it focuses on thinking patterns and how the thoughts we think shape our lives, as it did me. On Friday, January 4th, 2018, to be precise, I lost my job after many years of being a committed and high performing employee. If only losing my job was all I had to deal with, but it isn't. Month after month, I went on a downward spiral of one financial loss or the other due to bad monetary decisions, leaving me bankrupt from my years of hard work and savings – all in a bid to stay afloat until my next job comes. But the next job wasn't near in sight, and never came. To cap it up, I lost my mother to the cold hands of death, a mother I found great comfort in during times of difficulties, a mother I could share my problems with without feeling judged, a mother who gave me joy and a reason to keep pressing on through the travails of life, a mother who loved me unconditionally, a mother unreplaceable.

All these experiences made 2018 the worst year of my life, to say the least. I was depressed, experienced severe anxiety about everything, angry at life, and at having not only failed myself but my mother, who sacrificed so much to see me succeed in life. This even made me feel more emptiness, hopeless, lonely, and sad for 12 tough months. Though it seemed short, you may say, but it was the longest year of my life. I also developed suicidal tendencies and wished that death could come sooner. My depression became really bad that it dawned on me on December 1st, 2018, that I needed to get help from a therapist. Although the sessions I had with the therapist was an eye-opener on how much I had allowed my mistakes, failures, and losses to shape my way of thinking, how much I saw myself in a negative light, and how much all that happened isn't entirely my fault, I realized, however, that the ultimate power to reframe my negative thinking pattern into a more positive one lied with me. I also needed a strong reason why I needed to persevere through such tough times, a reason why I needed to win the battle for my mental health and wellbeing, and that reason came from the strength of my mother.

It is with this newfound realization that led me to journey on the road to recovery and today, having regained total control of my thoughts, feelings, and behaviors as well as my deep interest on the subject of CBT, I believe it is fair that I shared with you much of what I learned on the road to recovery as I know most of you reading this are probably going through a similar experience. To embark on this journey with me, I have enlisted the assistance of my friend, Dr. Lee Henton, a seasoned medical practitioner with broad knowledge on the subject of CBT as we share invaluable and life-saving hacks that could help you on your way to recovery, as well help a therapist or a counselor in their profession.

See you on the other side!

Section I

Understanding Cognitive Behavioral Therapy

Chapter 1

What is CBT?

Chances are you have heard of cognitive behavioral therapy (CBT), even if you are relatively unfamiliar with psychology. CBT is a common type of talk therapy that is globally practiced and very well used in the treatment of a wide range of conditions and mental health problems such as anxiety, depression, sleeping difficulties, drug, and alcohol abuse, and panic attacks among others – children, adolescents, adults, and older adults can all benefit from it.

In a lay man's term, CBT is based on the idea that how we think (cognition), how we feel (emotion) and how we act (behavior) are all interconnected. Specifically, what we think will determine our feelings and our behavior.

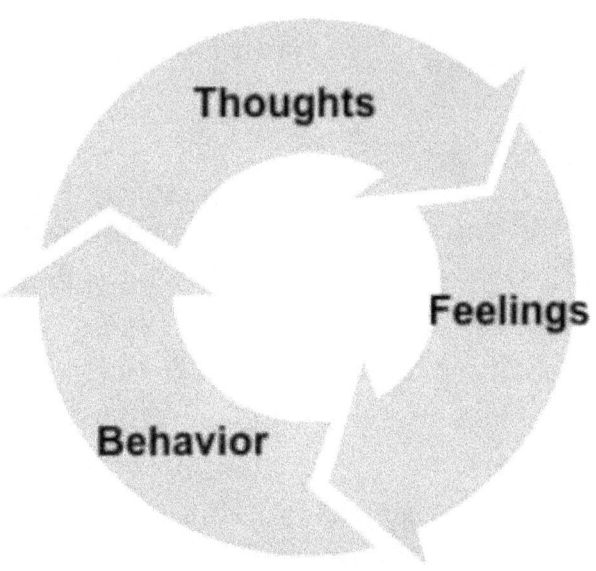

Figure 1: CBT Model

Cognitive Therapy

Cognitive therapy places emphasis on people's thoughts and how these thoughts affect their emotional, behavioral, and physiological responses to stressful situations. Often times, people have difficulty thinking rationally when they feel stressed and pressured by disturbing life experiences. Through cognitive therapy, you can identify and confront your thoughts about yourself, about the people around you, as well as the world around you.

Behavioral Therapy

In its most basic state, behavioral therapy is the encouragement of "patients to engage in adaptive behaviors and not to allow pathological internal experiences to dictate how they act" (Association for Behavioral and Cognitive Therapies, 2012). A person's negative reactions to normal stimuli are typically indicative of learned behaviors; this is because something negative occurred the last time the stimulus was present. Following a process known as extinction, therapists often try to change a person's negative reactions by letting them know that the negative result does not always happen with the stimulus. By following this process, the individual will more than likely positively engage in activities and behaviors if they have previously had positive outcomes. If the results of their activities and behaviors have been negative, then they are less likely to repeat such.

In most cases, psychotherapists who adopt the use of CBT in their practice often personalize and customize the therapy to suit the needs and personality of each person in their care. Have you ever interacted with a mental health therapist, a counselor, or even a psychiatry clinician in a professional setting? Then more than likely, you have participated in CBT. Perhaps your friends, families or loved ones have talked to you about how a mental health professional helped them in identifying unhelpful thoughts, patterns and behaviors, and how they were able to alter them to work towards their goals more effectively, then you have likewise, heard of the impacts of CBT.

In the list of tools used by psychologists when interacting with patients, CBT is one of such tools most frequently used. Though based on simple principles, the outcomes can be wildly positive when put into practice.

In this book, we will take a deeper dive into CBT, its inner workings, and how its principles, among many others, can be applied to improve your life. From this point on, I encourage you to keep a personal journal by your side as you continue reading to document your thoughts and responses as may be required.

A Short Trip Down History

To really understand the approach of cognitive behavioral therapy, it is important to know where it started from and in what reaction it was developed for. CBT emerged in the 1960s, in an era when psychological therapies were less known and practiced than they are today. Aaron T. Beck, a psychiatrist, is popularly credited as being the pioneer of CBT. However, the history of CBT would be incomplete without the mention of Albert Ellis, who, like Aaron Beck, was also developing a form of cognitive therapy at the same time as Beck. Ellis's work later became known as Rational Emotive Behavior Therapy (REBT).

At the time Aaron Beck discovered CBT, he was doing psychoanalysis, working at the University of Pennsylvania in the 1960s. During one of his many analytical sessions with his patients, Aaron observed that his patients displayed tendencies of **internal dialogue** going on in their minds — almost as though they were talking to themselves, but only reporting a fraction of this kind of thinking to him. For example, in a therapy session, the patient, thinking to herself, would mutter internally: "He (Aaron Beck) has not said much to me today. I wonder if he is angry with me?" These thoughts tend to create discomfort with the patient, making the patient feel a little bit anxious or perhaps annoyed. He or she could then respond to this thought with another thought: "He is likely tired, or perhaps I have not been talking about the things that are most important." The second thought most likely might change how the patient was feeling. Observing this with some of his patients, Beck realized that the link between *thoughts* and *feelings* was very important, which resulted in his invention of the term, **automatic thoughts** to describe emotion-filled thoughts that may pop up in the mind. Beck discovered that people were not always aware of such thoughts, but could, however, learn to identify and report them when they arise. Beck found that being able to identify these thoughts was the missing link to the patient understanding and overcoming his/ her problems or difficulties. It is because of the importance that was placed on thoughts that led Beck to call it cognitive therapy, which is now widely known as cognitive behavioral therapy (CBT) simply because the therapy uses behavioral techniques as well. CBT has since then, recorded successful scientific trials in several places by different teams, and has been applied to a variety of health problems.

Simultaneously, Albert Ellis was also working on a form of cognitive therapy that descended from the Stoic idea that it is not events that causes us distress, but the meaning we attribute to them. His ideas were developed as REBT. Although there is a huge overlap between both forms of therapy, Beckian cognitive therapy is unarguably the most influential and widely used form of therapy in the modern world.

How Does CBT Work?

CBT is a goal-oriented psychotherapy treatment that uses a practical, hands-on approach to problem-solving. CBT aims to change the thinking patterns and behaviors that are behind the difficulties people face, and by so doing, changing the way they feel. To change people's thinking patterns and their behaviors, CBT focuses on the thoughts, beliefs, attitudes, and images that are held (the cognitive processes of a person) and how these processes relate to how a person behaves, as a way of dealing with emotional problems.

It is noteworthy to mention that CBT is not designed for lifelong participation, but instead as a short term based therapy aimed to help people meet their goals in the near future. Most CBT treatment lasts somewhere around five to ten months, with patients attending a session per week, and with each session lasting for about 50 to 60-minute. During this time, the patient and therapist are working in collaboration to understand the underlying problems and developing new strategies for tackling them. A set of principles are introduced to the patients through CBT, which they can apply whenever they feel the need to, and that will last them for a lifetime.

For CBT to be effective, the therapist and the patient must both be invested in the process and willing to participate actively – which implies that both the therapist and the patient would need to work as a team to identify the problems the patient is facing, and come up with strategies to address them to create meaningful and positive solutions.

CBT is About Meanings

CBT is based on a model that it is not events in itself that makes us upset, but the meanings we attribute to them. As we live our lives, we interpret what goes on around us by forming *beliefs* and *understandings*. These meanings then go on to affect how we perceive the world. Take, for instance, if our thoughts are too negative, it can prevent us from doing things or seeing things that do not fit, that disconfirm what we believe to be true. In other words, we continue to cling on to the same old thoughts, failing to learn anything new.

Let's represent this analogy using an example. A depressed woman may say to herself, "I can not face going to work today: I just can't do it. Nothing will go right. I'll feel very awful." As a result of having and believing these thoughts, she may well ring in sick. By acting in such a way, she is not allowing herself to find out that her prediction might be wrong. She could have found some other things that she could do, that were at least okay, instead, she stays at home, brooding over her failure to go to work, and ending up thinking: "I have let everyone down. They will be mad at me. Why can't I do just as everyone else does? I'm too weak and worthless." She then ends up most probably feeling very worse, and having even more difficulty going to work the following day. Thinking, behaving, and feeling in such a way like this could trigger the start of a downward spiral. Note that this vicious thought circle applies to several kinds of problems and negative thoughts encountered in our everyday lives.

The figure below paints an illustration of how we give meanings to events and the outcome that results.

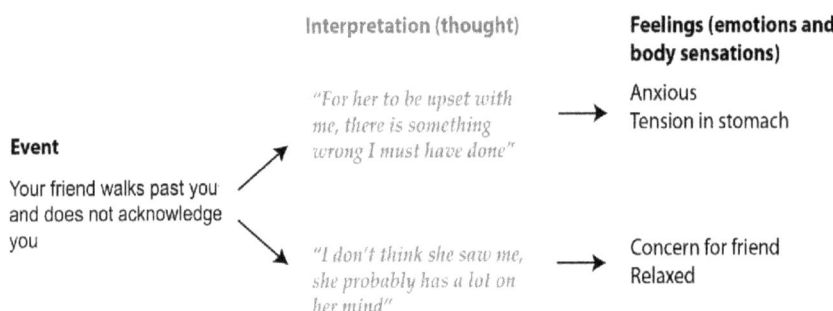

Figure 2: Our interpretation of events determines our feelings toward them.

In the first interpretation, the events are personalized (*"What have I done wrong?"*), which then results in feelings of anxious sensations. However, the second interpretation tends to understand the friend's behavior in a more neutral term, resulting in a different outcome from the first interpretation.

Take a look at another example below

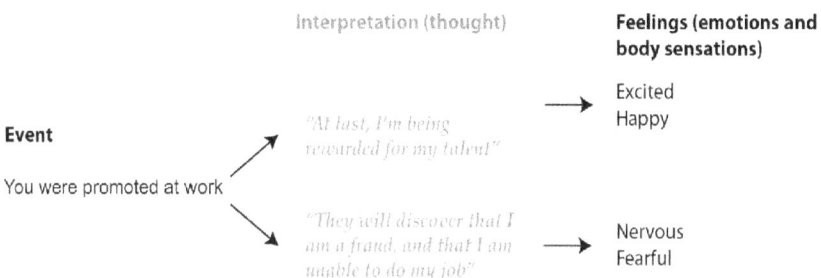

Figure 3: Another example of how our interpretation of events determines how we feel about them.

The first interpretation (the offer of promotion) is an excited one – which is viewed as a welcome opportunity. The second interpretation, however, is less exciting and positive – the person offered a promotion is making a negative prediction of what is likely to happen, resulting in anxiety.

The idea of how we interpret events did not start today. Nearly 2000 years ago, Epictetus, the Greek philosopher said:

"Men are disturbed, not by things, but by the principles and notions which they form concerning things." —**Epictetus**

In 1602, Shakespeare said something similar:

"There is nothing either good or bad, but thinking makes it so." —Shakespeare

How we interpret events may not be a new idea; however, it is a powerful one. It explains why some people are excited at the opportunity singing in front of a crowd (*"At last, my talent will be recognized!"*) whereas, for some other persons, it is a terrifying feeling (*"I will make a fool of myself and everyone will laugh at me!"*).

We may not always be able to change the situations we find ourselves in (or perhaps the people we meet); however, we are responsible and in charge of how we interpret events. How we decide to handle a situation, and the perspective we choose to take would determine how we feel. That being said, have at the back of your mind that CBT may not provide a cure to your condition or make an unpleasant situation go away, but it most definitely can give you the power that you need to cope with your situation in a healthy way and in a way that helps you feel better about yourself and your life.

A survivor of the Nazi death camps, Viktor Frankl, rendered one of his most powerful words on this:

"Everything can be taken from a man but one thing: the last of the human freedoms – to choose one's attitude in any given set of circumstances, to choose one's own way." — **Frankl**

Where Do These Negative Thoughts Come From?

As suggested by Aaron Beck, these thinking patterns are set up in childhood, becoming automatic and relatively fixed. So, for instance, a child who did not experience much open affection from his/her parents but instead, well praised for school work, might start to think, "I must do well all the time. If I don't, I will be rejected." Such a rule for living (which is termed, a **dysfunctional assumption**) may work well for the person most of the time and may even help them work harder. However, if something happens that is out of their control, and they experience setbacks or failure, then the dysfunctional thought pattern could be triggered. This person may then start to have **automatic thoughts** such as, "I have totally failed. No one will like me again. I can't face them."

Cognitive behavioral therapy acts to help the person understand that "this is what is going on." It aims to help him/ her step outside their automatic thoughts and test them out. For the depressed woman scenario earlier discussed, CBT would encourage that she examines real-life experiences to see what would happen to her, or to others in a similar situation. Then, in the light of a more realistic perspective, she may be willing to take the chance to test out what other people would think, by revealing her difficulties to friends, families or loved ones.

It should be made clear that negative things can and do happen. But when we are in a distorted state of mind, our predictions and interpretations may be based on a biased view of the situation, thus making it difficult to face them, and even worse, difficult in addressing them from a holistic perspective. CBT helps people to correct these misinterpretations.

The role of a CBT therapist thus is to help you understand and examine your beliefs and help you to make sense of meanings.

CBT as a Doing Therapy

CBT is a great way to understand what keeps a problem going and when armed with the information, our sole job is to take action to get unstuck from the problem. What makes CBT much different is that it is not just a 'talking therapy.' Psychologists have found that for CBT to be really helpful in making changes in your life, it is best to think of it as a 'doing therapy.'

Doing Homework

Working on homework assignments between sessions is a crucial part of the CBT process. However, what this may entail will vary. For instance, at the beginning of the therapy, you might be asked to keep a diary of any incidents that may stir up feelings of anxiety or depression, so that the thoughts surrounding the incident can be examined. You could also be given another assignment later on in the therapy, made up of exercises that will help you cope with problem situations of a specific kind.

Why Do I Need to Do Homework?

People willing to do home assignments get the most benefit from CBT. For instance, most people who suffer from depression say they don't want to take part in work or social activities until they feel better. CBT then introduces them to an alternative viewpoint – that attempting some activity of this nature, albeit small to begin with, will help make them feel better.

Now, if that individual is open to the idea to test this out, he/ she could agree to meet a friend for a drink at the pub. By being open to partaking in a social activity like this, they tend to make faster progress compared to someone who feels unable to take this risk.

Who Can CBT Help?

CBT has been found to be most suitable for people with a particular and identifiable problem that is addressable with specific tasks and goals. CBT's practical nature makes it useful for people looking for a hands-on approach to their treatment. Originally, CBT was developed to be used as a treatment option for depression, but it quickly became adapted to successfully treat people with several health conditions ranging from anxiety to chronic pain and addiction.

CBT as a tool can be used in treating people suffering from mental health problems and other health conditions such as:

- Depression.
- Anxiety (including generalized anxiety disorder, panic attacks, and panic disorder, and social anxiety disorder)
- Post-traumatic stress disorder (PTSD) and dissociative disorders such as depersonalization and derealization
- Obsessive compulsive disorder (OCD)
- Eating disorders including anorexia nervosa and bulimia nervosa
- Personality disorders
- Psychosis and unusual beliefs
- Low self-esteem
- Physical health problems, including chronic pain, and tinnitus
- Medically unexplained symptoms including fatigue and seizures
- Substance and drug use disorders
- Sleep disorders
- Phobias and;
- Sexual disorders

CBT (together with medication) is rapidly generating interest in treating people suffering from hallucinations and delusions, and those with long-term health problems such as irritable bowel syndrome (IBS) and arthritis. Using CBT (a short term therapy) in treating problems that are severely disabling and more long term is less easy to accomplish. Although CBT cannot cure the physical symptoms of these health problems, people can, however, learn its principles to help them cope better with their symptoms, improve their quality of life and increase their chances of making further progress.

CBT Principles – What is CBT Like?

Although therapy must be adapted to suit each person, there are, however, certain principles that underlie cognitive behavior therapy for everyone. Ultimately, CBT aims to teach you to be your own therapist, by helping you understand your current ways of thinking and behaving, and by equipping you with the tools needed to change your maladaptive cognitive and behavioral patterns. Some of the core principles of CBT to guide you along are:

CBT is problem-focused: By remaining focused on the problems you and your therapist identifies, it becomes much easier to produce clear treatment goals and objectives.

CBT emphasizes active participation and collaboration: You and your therapist will work in unison in actively seeking out ways to help with your problem, which may include going into the world to seek other people's input, setting goals, and developing a treatment plan. You may also be required to create your homework assignments. You and your therapist's active participation and collaboration are key during therapy; without it, the goal-oriented and problem-focused approach would be ineffective.

CBT is focused on the present: Since CBT is present-focused such as the feelings of anxiety or depression you feel 'now,' your current problems are therefore discussed. Although there may be some mention of your personal history, past thoughts or behaviors to understand the origin of your problems, beliefs, and interpretations, therapy often occurs with a focus on the here and now of the problems causing you pain and suffering – and this is where you and your therapist have the power to make changes.

CBT sessions are well structured: The structure of sessions will relatively remain constant for the period of treatment. You and the therapist will set a plan and address all the items on the list every week. This approach allows the relationship between you and your therapist to deepen, which is also a core principle of CBT.

CBT is a time-limited approach: CBT sessions are usually short-term, typically between 6 and 20 sessions compared to other forms of therapy that can last for years. This does not imply that CBT treatment is less effective than other forms of therapy – it actually tends to out-perform them.

CBT emphasizes relapse prevention: Learning to stay well is an important part of CBT. By understanding the factors that triggered your anxiety, depression, or any other issues, you can then be able to quickly identify and immobilize warning signs of a relapse when they resurface.

How Effective is CBT?

CBT is an evidence-based form of therapy in which researchers figure out *what* components of therapy is best suited to work, for *which* problems, and *why*. Therapy sessions conducted on an individual basis also pay close attention to evidence: CBT patients are often encouraged to set personal goals (e.g., *"If I were feeling less anxious, do shopping by myself without the need to escape would be a walk in the park for me"*) and then record the data (evidence) about if these goals are being met.

When the question *"how effective is CBT?"* is asked, it means *"what is it effective for?"* and *"effective compared to what?"* There is also a need to examine *"how often the conditions get better by themselves?"*. One way researchers address these questions is by performing what is called randomized controlled trials (RCTs) —where different treatments are systematically and carefully compared to each other. This is the same process applied in medicine to test the effectiveness and safeness of new drugs. In the past few decades, CBT has been examined by thousands of such studies, and researchers can now combine the results of these RCTs to demonstrate in more reliable ways, which treatments are best suited to work. The chart below depicts the result of a meta-analysis of CBT published in 2015. The results were pulled from a total of 48 studies that compared CBT with 'treatment as usual' for close to 7000 people that suffer from anxiety, depression, or mixed anxiety & depression. The results clearly show that CBT is a more favored treatment option, i.e., when compared to their usual treatment, more people become better when they get treated with CBT.

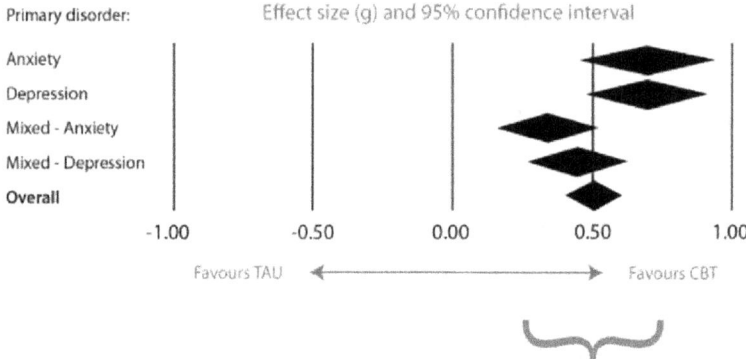

Figure 4: CBT's effectiveness vs. treatment as usual (TAU)

Another way to measure the effectiveness of CBT in treating psychological problems is by taking a look at the 'response rates.' A person is said to 'respond' to therapy if their symptoms have significantly improved by the end of treatment. The chart below depicts the CBT response rates across a wide variety of conditions based on a study of 106 meta-analyses published in 2012.

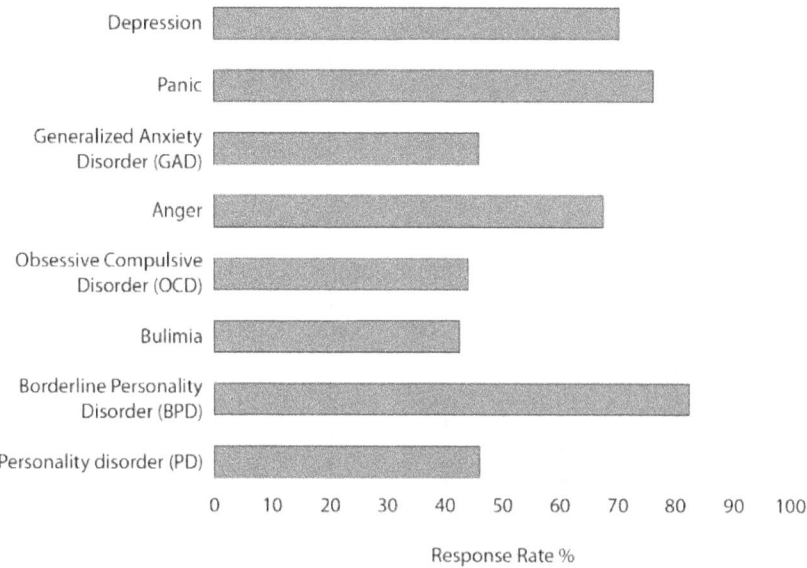

Figure 5: CBT response rates for a variety of conditions (the higher, the better).

I know what you are thinking; "these results are looking good," right? but you may want to ask, *"What do the results look like for the alternatives?"* That same study also compared the CBT response rates to other 'genuine' treatment as usual or forms of therapy. Based on the analysis conducted, it was determined that CBT for depression was as effective as medication or other forms of psychotherapy, but more effective than treatment as usual. CBT for anxiety it was discovered was more effective when compared to other forms of genuine therapies and was credited as a "reliable first-line approach in treating this class of disorders."

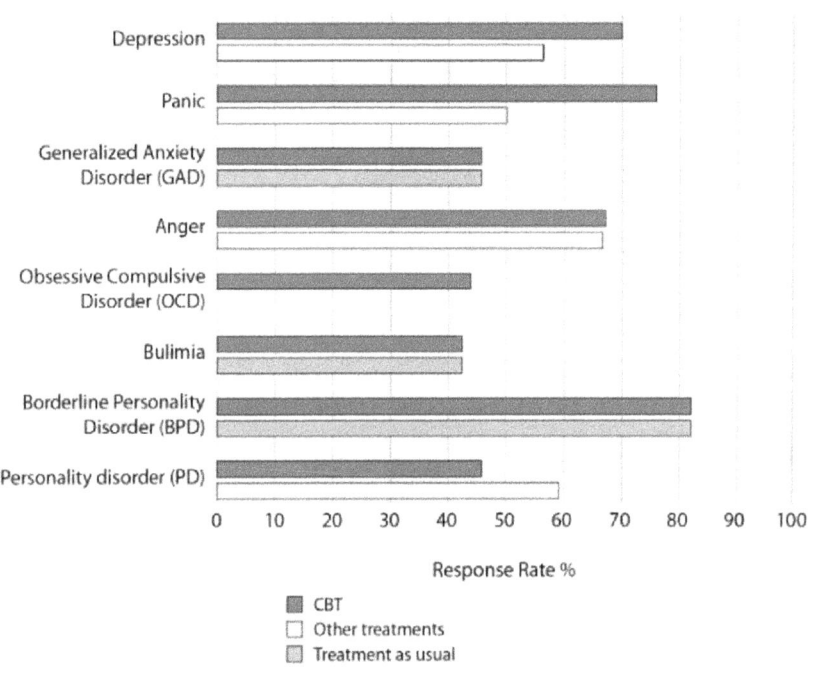

Figure 6: CBT response rates compared to other treatments or treatment as usual.

The overall summary from the reviews, as mentioned above, is that for many conditions, CBT is as effective or more effective when compared to other genuine forms of therapy and better, compared to treatment as usual (which mostly includes check-ups with doctors or use of medications) or doing nothing.

How is CBT Administered?

It is widely recognized that a few patient-therapist face-face sessions of CBT can, for instance, be very helpful in treating people suffering from anxiety and depression. However, not many people can readily have access to a CBT therapist—perhaps there is none within their immediate reach, not covered in their insurance network, or they are costly to afford. It may also be that taking time off from paid work or child care each week to see a therapist can be difficult.

If, for example, you want to try CBT for anxiety or depression and you are unable to see a CBT therapist, take heart, for you may not need to. There are several options through which CBT can be administered without a therapist, which includes self-help books and online-based treatment. Many studies show that self-directed CBT can be very effective.

For example, a review of 33 studies shows that treatment via self-help resulted in significant reductions in anxiety; another review of 34 studies on depression showed similar results, especially when the treatments involved the use of CBT techniques. On average, both reviews found that the self-help treatments were moderately helpful. In other words, people who undertook the self-help treatment felt substantially better—maybe not 100% better, but were noticeably less anxious and depressed.

It is also suggested from these data that people who do self-help CBT for anxiety and depression tend to maintain their progress over a period of time – this shows that people who learn CBT skills on their own can apply the skills to keep feeling better, thus fulfilling one of the major principles of CBT which is to "be your own therapist." Well, I can tell you for a fact that during one of my mental episodes from anxiety and depression, self-help treatments was my regular companion, because although I first had a few in-person therapy sessions with a therapist, it became ultimately expensive to sustain especially as I was out of a job at the time. Overall, I quickly learned to use self-help formats (CBT books and its workbook companion, motivational and inspirational self-help books, etc.), all of which helped me in learning the skills necessary to become my own therapist against anxiety and depression.

But what does this even mean for in-person therapy? Does this mean the end for therapists? Absolutely not. Self-help treatment can likewise be done with limited input from a therapist—for example, a brief phone call every week—which can serve as an extra boost compared to self-help alone. The additional benefit of working with a therapist comes from not only having an expert's input but also having someone who cares and provides constant encouragement.

Although the above statement holds, it should be noted, however, that self-help CBT is most suitable for those with mild to moderate symptoms and generally capable of functioning properly. A severely depressed person who is unable to get out of bed, for instance, is likely not a good match and will most probably need to have a one-on-one treatment with a therapist.

Should you choose to pursue self-help CBT, then:

- Get a book that resonates with you. People are drawn to different methods, level of detail, tones, etc. If you feel the book is a good fit, there is a higher chance you will stay engaged with it.

- Choose a book based on solid research. Self-help therapy takes a considerable amount of time and effort, so it is advisable to channel your focus toward a program with a solid grounding.

- Create a room in your schedule to go through the program. Therapy of any kind can be tackled at better and worse times. While the likelihood exists that you will always have competing activities, you should avoid times when you are truly overextended to prevent the therapy from being pushed aside or postponed.

- Follow the program as carefully as possible. It is very easy to skip parts of a self-help program that we think would not work, or that we think we already know. One of the dangers of skipping parts of a self-help program is that if you find a program that does not work, you would not know if it is because it was not the right fit for you or because you only did part of it. Following through with the instructions is the best way to benefit and know what actually works for you.

On the flip side, CBT can also be delivered through an online medium in several ways. This can be via a video chat program, e.g., Skype, which is very similar to in-person therapy, with the difference being that both the patient and therapist are miles apart. Computer-based CBT, SMS, Emails, and other online chat media can also be used to administer CBT. Essentially, all these methods use the internet as a means of delivery, which is somewhat similar to what a person may receive with in-person treatment.

A common question about online CBT is if it is as effective as in-person therapy. As earlier mentioned, video chat/ conferencing, for instance, is quite similar to traditional in-person therapy, and it is expected to work equally well. However, a completely automated online CBT treatment, designed by expert clinicians, will almost surely perform way better than in-person treatment program administered by a therapist that is poorly trained. In some ways, I believe the question: "Which is better?" misses the mark.

These systems of CBT treatment does address a critical need in modern mental health treatment. Several people around the world would benefit tremendously from evidence-based techniques such as CBT. However, if for a reason or another, they cannot access in-person services, self-help, and online CBT, including fully automated-computerized CBT, would be their best bet.

The summary of all this is to discover what works best for you, given the peculiarity of your problem, your financial position, insurance coverage as well as your accessibility to in-person therapy.

What Types of CBT Are There?

Certain forms of CBT exercise greater emphasis on the role our thinking plays on feelings and behaviors, while others may focus on the influence of environmental factors. Whichever the case is, the type of CBT that is best suited for you will be determined by the nature of your difficulties, the outcome of previous therapies (if any), your unique background, your preferences, and your unique strengths and weaknesses.

Several types of CBT have been designed over the years. However, I will discuss some of the well-known types of CBT used in the modern world as well as their applications.

- **Cognitive Therapy (CT):** As already mentioned, cognitive therapy was developed by Aaron T. Beck, which was one of the earliest therapies considered as Cognitive Behavior Therapy. Beck hypothesized the Beck Cognitive Triad, which included three types of cognitive distortions that he proposed caused and maintained depressive episodes. These cognitive distortions are about the self, the world, and the future. Take, for instance, a depressed patient who enters therapy with negative thoughts such as, "I am worthless (self)," "people don't seem to like me, and I am bad at doing my job well enough (world)," and things will never change (future)." In particular, negative views about the future can be very problematic because they relate to hopelessness, which in most cases, stands as a risk factor for suicide.

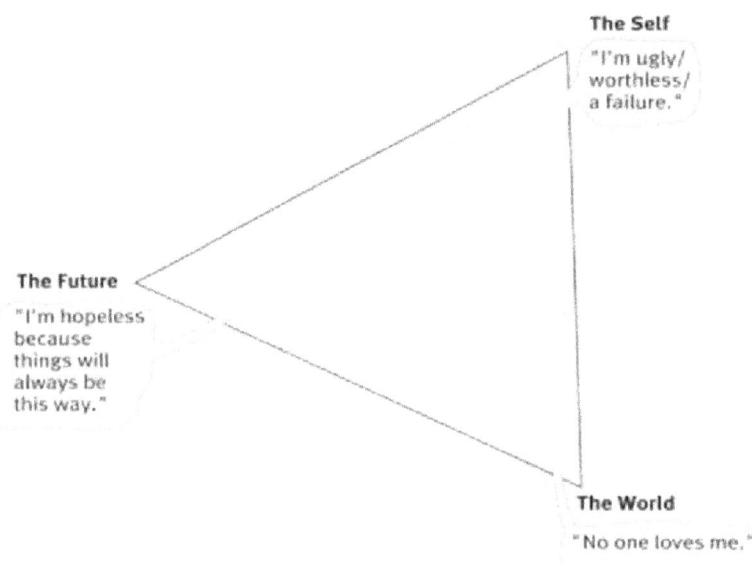

Figure 7

Cognitive therapy was originally designed to treat depression, i.e., major depressive disorder, but has since gained clinical success in reducing anxiety. It is also shown to be an excellent treatment option for people with phobias, generalized anxiety disorder, and ADHD.

Generally speaking, the goal of CT is to spot faulty lines of thinking and reduce irrational thoughts. CT is known for challenging toxic thinking and replacing unhealthy thoughts with more logical and rational ones.

- **Rational Emotive Behavior Therapy (REBT):** Just like Cognitive Therapy, REBT is another earlier form of cognitive behavioral therapy, founded in the 1950s by Albert Ellis that shares some similarities with CT. REBT emphasizes on a patient's irrational beliefs and actively targeting them for a change into more rational ones. To support the use of REBT in treatments, Ellis developed a model called the ABC Technique of Irrational Beliefs. According to this model, Ellis believes the activating event (**A**) is not what causes negative emotional and behavioral consequences (**C**), but instead it is the unrealistic interpretation that a person attributes to the events that result to an irrational belief system (**B**) that helps in causing the consequences (**C**).

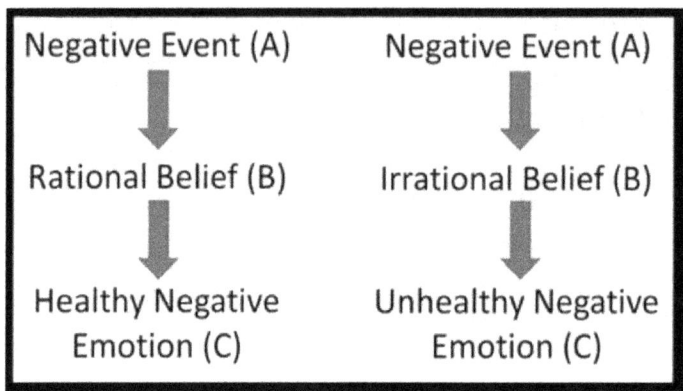

Figure 8

Let's represent the above analogy using an example. Gina is upset because she had bad grades in her math test. The Activating event, A, in this case, is that she had bad grades. Her Belief, B, is that for her not to be seen as worthless, she must have good grades. The Consequence, C, of A and B, is that Gina feels depressed.

Through REBT, Gina, with the help of a therapist, can then identify and confront her irrational beliefs and expectations, e.g., I must be perfect, or I must have good grades to be worthwhile. The therapist would then help Gina to understand that no evidence exists that to be worthwhile, she must have good grades, or that getting bad grades is awful. He would make her see reason that although she desires good grades, which would be good to have, the absence of it, however, would hardly make her worthless.

After confronting Gina's negative thinking by **reframing** it, Gina and the therapist then developed a realistic thinking, which then helped her in developing more rational beliefs and healthy coping strategies. It was only when this was accomplished that Gina was able to change her negative thinking and unrealistic beliefs.

It is this confrontation of Gina's irrational thinking into more rational ones that the ABC model is most often being referred to as the ABCD Model. In this revised model, the D stands for the Disputation of Beliefs. Disputation is not an original member of the ABC Model because it takes place outside of the ABC.

- **Dialectical Behavior Therapy (DBT):** DBT is a behavioral therapy that is also a form of cognitive behavioral therapy. Marsha Linehan originally developed DBT for the treatment of people with the most complex type of syndromes, e.g., borderline personality disorder or impulsive and suicidal behaviors. It is based on a dialectical philosophy that challenges us to confront and make peace with the complex and opposite truths that are often inherent in most situations, the most basic being accepting ourselves or changing ourselves. DBT is a skill-based approach that combines cognitive behavioral techniques with the core skill practice, mindfulness (a non-judgmental, present-centered intentional awareness), and then applying this mindful awareness to life through other major DBT skills such as distress tolerance, interpersonal skills, and emotion regulation. This has proven to shown great results, where other treatments have failed and have since been successfully applied to several problems where dysregulation of emotions and destructive impulsivity interrupted normal living. Mental health disorders where DBT treatment has been applied aside personality problems include eating disorders, depression, and anxiety. It has also been used in treating alcohol and drug abuse as well as explosive anger.

- **Acceptance and Commitment Therapy (ACT):** This form of cognitive behavior therapy for anxiety and other mood-related problems was developed in the 1980s by Steven Hayes, building on ideas from radical behaviorism. Unlike traditional CBT (CBT-interventions based on the idea that our thoughts influence our emotions and behaviors), ACT does not emphasize changing, challenging, or replacing disturbing thoughts, but instead, focuses on the relationship we have with our thoughts by exploring other ways to react differently to how we think. Have you ever noticed that when you are anxious about something, it becomes worsened when you attempt to eradicate the thoughts, engage in over-controlling behaviors or strict, rigid forms of coping? Well, I know this because I experienced it during one of my emotional breakdown episodes. ACT aims to increase psychological flexibility, i.e., the ability to Accept your reactions, to Choose a valued direction, and to Take action (ACT).

In Acceptance and Commitment Therapy, mindfulness and other ACT exercises are used to break the "living in the past or future" habit and to commit to living in the present moment. Even traditional CBT proposes that anxiety stems from thoughts about the future, while depression is mostly fueled by thoughts focused on the past.

In general, ACT helps us see our old thoughts and ourselves from a different perspective, which then gives us the opportunity to act in new ways around our old thoughts.

- **Cognitive Processing Therapy (CPT):** CPT, developed by psychologist, Patricia Resick, has been shown to treat Post-traumatic Stress Disorder (PTSD) successfully. Military veterans and sexual assault or rape victims form part of the populations of PTSD on which CPT is shown to be an effective form of psychotherapy. Like several forms of CBT, the CPT therapist works to build strong therapeutic rapport, which is especially crucial for PTSD patients that often have safety and trust issues when asked to recall memories about traumatic events. CPT also involves psychoeducation about PTSD; this is to help PTSD patients understand how PTSD symptoms develop and are maintained. During therapy, the patient documents an account of the traumatic experience, and via therapeutic exchanges with the therapist, they become able to identify the specific cognitive distortions present in their belief system. By doing this, they learn how to challenge these cognitive distortions, which, according to theorists, may exacerbate shame, anger, and anxiety, thereby leading to patients avoiding reminders of the traumatic events.

As patients allow more realistic adaptive beliefs, they begin to overtake the cognitive distortions, helping them decrease the behaviors of avoidance, thus leading to reductions both in emotional symptoms and increase in healthy behaviors such as returning to work, a more regular sleep schedule, or increased emotional and physical intimacy, etc. CPT, which combines exposure therapy (a technique used by CBT therapists) as well as cognitive techniques from CBT, has been incorporated by the United States Veteran's Administration into several of their programs to help military veterans who suffer from PTSD.

- **Mindfulness-Based Cognitive Therapy (MBCT):** Developed by psychologists John Teasdale, Zinden Segal, and Mark Williams, MBCT combined the knowledge and techniques of CBT with mindfulness meditation practices. MBCT's most strongest evidence is as a relapse-prevention treatment for people that suffer from depression. That being said, research from scientific studies suggests that MBCT is a very effective form of therapy for people living with high degrees of anxiety, chronic pain, stress, and gastrointestinal problems like IBS (intestinal bowel syndrome). Likewise, it can be very effective in helping people that experience panic attacks, and that includes depersonalization. The goal of MBCT is not to change one's thoughts but changing how a person reacts to his/her thoughts, thus helping to make healthy choices with each given day and improve life on a moment to moment basis. This type of cognitive approach breaks the spiral of negative toxic thinking, which can worsen emotions such as anxiety and depression.

Pros and Cons of CBT

The approach to CBT does have its advantages and disadvantages. Just like any other therapy, there is always a risk of negative emotion from a traumatic event or experience resurfacing. Let's take a look at what's good and what may hold back progress in treatment, which both the therapist and you, the patient, should be aware of and discuss before or during therapy; Some of which we have already discussed in the preceding pages.

Here is a list of pros:

- One important advantage of cognitive behavioral therapy is that it is designed to be short, ranging from five to ten months when compared to other "talking" therapies.
- CBT can help treat some mental health disorders where it has shown that medication alone has not helped improve symptoms.
- CBT focuses on changing thoughts and behaviors to change how you feel.
- CBT strategies are practical and helpful and can help people in coping with future stresses.

- CBT can help improve emotional processing as well as the quality of life.
- CBT can be provided in several formats such as face-to-face, online, self-help, or even via workbooks. It can likewise be useful in a group setting.
- CBT is useful for all age groups.

Here is a list of cons:

- You have to commit to the process. The therapist has no magic wand to wave that will take away your problems without co-operation.
- CBT emphasizes the capacity of an individual to change their thoughts, feelings, and behaviors and does not address broader problems in families, systems, or environments that could significantly impact their health and wellbeing.
- For people who suffer from severe mental health challenges or with a learning disability, CBT could prove more difficult as a treatment option.
- As CBT addresses the sources of depression, anxiety, or other stress-causing emotions, you may initially feel uncomfortable when exposed to this type of treatment.

- The possible underlying causes of negative emotions are not wholly addressed with the CBT treatment as it emphasizes more on the present problems.
- In real life, while doing the actual work, it could take some time for you to reclaim your mental health and improve your quality of life.

Chapter 2

What Does CBT Involve?

Typically, a patterned, step-wise approach is most times followed when administering CBT. Although the process described herein is linear in fashion, bear in mind that people and the problems they face are not always straightforward, often calling for a 'dance' to and fro between the steps.

Step 1: Identifying the Problem and Setting Goals

During the first few sessions, a CBT therapist wants to uncover the kind of problems troubling you, his patient. This may include issues such as a medical condition, grief, anger, divorce, or symptoms of a mental health disorder. In addition, they will want to explore your goals, i.e., what do you want differently at the end of therapy. To conduct an assessment of your problems, the CBT therapist, will discuss some or all of the following:

- Asking open-ended questions so that you can discuss your problems, e.g., *"Tell me why you are here,"* or *"What has been troubling you of late?"*

- Making a 'problem list' alongside with you and brainstorming together about the relative importance of the individual problems, e.g., *"Now that a list of the things troubling you at the moment has been made, could we try putting the individual problem in the order of how they interfere with the life you desire to lead?"*

- Generating goals that are SMART. Often, this is achieved by focusing on the behaviors you want to change, e.g., *"I want to stop experiencing panic attacks at least three weeks after the end of therapy."* In my book, **How to Stop Overthinking**, I discussed in-depth how you can set effective SMART goals.

- Using structured interviews and questionnaires to determine the presence or absence of symptoms and difficulties, e.g., *"I would ask you a number of questions about your feelings in the past month, and I would like that you answered each question with this five-point scale that goes from 'never' to 'very often'"*

- Asking questions relating to risk, which includes discussing current and past suicidal thoughts and actions, e.g., *"Do you ever have the thoughts of hurting yourself or ending your life?"*

Step 2: Identifying Core Beliefs About the Problems

It is not enough to identify a problem, we also need to find solutions to the problem. In finding solutions to the problem, it is important to understand what keeps the problem going and find some ways to put a stop to it. In understanding what keeps a problem and stopping it, we first need to understand what core beliefs are.

What are Core Beliefs?

Core beliefs are nothing but deep-seated assumptions, underlying ideas, or thoughts you hold about yourself, others, and the world, which over a period of time, you come to believe as true. However, they are mostly developed from our early childhood experiences, which, for most people, does not reflect what is actually true. These beliefs then turn out to impact our feelings, our relationship with others, and our lives in general.

Core beliefs can be positive or negative, but for the examples going forward, we would dwell more on the negative side and how it can be reframed to become positive.

Typically, core beliefs fit into one of the following:

I am _____

People are _____

The world is _____

Below are some examples of negative core beliefs:

- I am ugly and up to no good
- Everyone else does well at their job than I do
- The world is full of greedy and self-centered people

These are all core beliefs. Such inner beliefs dictate our whole lives, which in most cases, are wrong. Negative, and often inaccurate core beliefs like those mentioned above, will drastically lower your chances of experiencing joy and self-fulfillment in life.

How Core Beliefs Develop

Let me describe a clinical example of how core beliefs develop. David's childhood was characterized by how much his parents were very critical and placed great emphasis on academic excellence. His brother excelled academically, but often, he struggled to meet the high standards of his parents. Due to this reason, David developed the core belief, *"I am useless,"* and whenever he fails a test, he develops the automatic thought, *"I am a total failure."*

While core beliefs can be helpful in some cases, most times, they could cause negative emotions. For instance, it has been suggested that people experiencing symptoms of depression are more likely to have core beliefs telling them they are helpless and/ or unloveable. People with anxiety, on the other hand, are more likely to have core beliefs telling them the world is not a safe place. If you suffer from depression, anxiety, or any other conditions, examining your core beliefs would help you and your therapist to understand what keeps your problem up and running and what to do to put an end to it.

In the subsequent sections, I would walk you through how to identify and analyze your core beliefs.

Identifying Core Beliefs

Identifying problematic core beliefs first starts with learning to identify those thoughts that keep bouncing around in your head each day. These thoughts are called *automatic thoughts* simply because they arise and pop into our heads without consciously thinking about them. At this point, you should be aware that core beliefs can lead to automatic negative thoughts

There are two ways you can identify your automatic thoughts. The first is to sit quietly and observe your thoughts. This can be done at any time, but this technique can be found most helpful when you are feeling down and anxious for a while. Note that the idea is not to ponder if these thoughts are right or wrong or true or false but to simply identify the thoughts.

The other way you can identify your automatic thoughts is to recall the times your feelings or emotions shifted abruptly, like when you were angry, anxious, sad, etc. Again, the goal is not to ruminate on the thoughts, we only want to identify them as thoughts, while noting the content. Once these thoughts have been identified, it is very helpful to note them in a thought record. In your thought record, ensure you keep track of:

- The situation, e.g., You did not get the job
- The feelings or emotions you felt, e.g., Anger (at yourself) and Sadness (about not getting the job)
- The automatic thoughts you had, noting them as accurately as possible (This will help you identify distortions in your thoughts vs. facts), e.g., I will always be the second or third choice.

The next step is to use the automatic thoughts noted to drill down to the underlying core beliefs. One of the most powerful techniques used to identify core beliefs is the *downward arrow question and answer technique*. Essentially, this technique aims to ask you questions about your automatic thoughts, which, for every question, has an answer.

By asking questions, therapists can help you to identify your core beliefs through negative automatic thoughts. A series of negative thoughts will be generated until you reach the core belief.

Here are some sample questions this technique uses:
- What went through your mind then?
- What does this imply to you?
- What do others say about this?

Below is an example of the Downward Arrow Question and Answer Technique in action:

Joe submits his application for a job and receives a call that the position is filled. His first thought is: "I knew it, I did not get the job."

Joe notes this thought when he realizes he is feeling sad and angry several days after the call. So, he questioned himself, "What does this thought imply about me?"

⬇

He concludes: "It means I never got the job." And "I will always be the second or third choice."

⬇

He then questions himself, "What is the worst thing about not being selected?"

⬇

He learns that "It implies I am not good enough."

⬇

He then asks, "Why am I so upset about this?"

⬇

He concludes that it means "I am not worthy of a good job."

⬇

The underlying core belief of Joe is, "I am not worthy."

Joe realizes that he has a strong negative reaction that has gone on for a while. Not only does he feel bad about his core belief, but it could also make him less likely to apply for another position. Therefore, Joe needs to understand the reason for having so much trouble in this situation. Without first identifying his core belief, Joe would be unable to understand nor change it.

One last example:

Jane expresses feelings of helplessness and worthlessness because her daughter has declined to clean her room. Below is an example of the Q & A technique that is applied to Jane's automatic thought to identify her core belief.

Automatic Thought	This room is a mess.
Question: Answer:	What does that mean to me? She's a slob!
Question: Answer:	Why is that so bad assuming that's true? My friends may see how messy her room is when they come over
Question: Answer:	Why is that so bad? They will think I am an inadequate mother
Question: Answer:	Why is that so bad assuming that's true? I will feel worthless if my friends disapprove of me = **CORE BELIEF!**

In general, once you and your therapist have identified problematic core beliefs, your therapist will encourage you to discuss your thoughts about them. This may require that you observe what you tell yourself of an experience (self-talk), interpreting the meaning of a situation, and your beliefs about yourself, others, and the world.

Step 3: Analyzing Core Beliefs by Identifying Cognitive Distortions

In reaching your core belief, you have assumed each answer is true along the way. The key is to recognize that the automatic core beliefs are not necessarily true by asking yourself if they are accurate. If you find negative core beliefs that hold you back, you need to consider where they may have originated from.

Do you hear the voice of a parent from an ugly experience of your childhood?

Are you hearing the echoes of a partner that pulled you down by undermining your self-esteem?

The above are mere examples.

Finding the origins of your core beliefs can help you identify cognitive distortions in each answer provided in each question. This is the first step to changing your core beliefs. Your therapist or counselor can help you with this process if you are really struggling with it. Analyzing your core beliefs is not easy, but doing so can help you root out negative and inaccurate thought patterns. After you have determined the origin of your core beliefs, go through your answers such as that in step 2 above, and look for cognitive distortions.

Note: Depending on the nature of the core beliefs and the circumstances surrounding it, it may be impracticable to associate your core beliefs with an origin. In such a case, simply look for cognitive distortions from each answer provided.

What are Cognitive Distortions?

Cognitive distortions or unhelpful thinking styles are inaccurate ways of thinking, which may seem true, accurate, or real.

Sometimes, our brains take 'short cuts' in generating results that are not entirely accurate. Different cognitive short cuts lead to several kinds of bias or distortions in how we think. Sometimes we jump to the worst conclusion possible, while at other times, we hold ourselves responsible for things that are not our fault. Cognitive distortions are prevalent amongst everyone, automatic, completely normal, and not our fault. A study suggests that people develop cognitive distortions as a survival method in coping with adverse life events. Unless we learn to identify them when they arise and contain them, the effects it could have on our moods and lives can be very powerful. By understanding the different types of cognitive distortions, you are on the way to spotting the thinking traps that hold you back.

Types of Cognitive Distortions

To help you get started in spotting your cognitive distortions, below are some of the key thought habits generally known to cause distress, which also includes anxiety and depression. You can take a cue from the examples to spot your cognitive distortions:

Jumping to conclusions: It is when you predict the outcome of a situation will turn out badly without holistically looking at all the possible scenarios.

E.g., He did not call me; he wants to break up with me.

Blaming: You play the victim mentality by blaming others or yourself for the problems in your life while giving up control of your feelings.

E.g., He makes me so miserable!

All or Nothing Thinking: You see things in black or white terms, with no shades of gray. If you make a mistake, you see yourself as a failure.

E.g., I am a bad mother

Disqualifying the Positive: In a given situation, instead of just ignoring the positive aspects or filtering it out, you further dismiss it as a fluke, argue against it, or focus on the negative.

E.g., Although she asked that I mentor a coworker due to my competence, she has no idea that I really do not know a lot

Emotional Reasoning: You lose objectivity of the facts by sticking to the interpretations of yourself based on your emotions and negative self-image.

E.g., I feel like a stupid person, so I must be a stupid person.

Fallacy of Fairness: You expect life to be fair.

E.g., I should get what I deserve because life should be fair.

Fortune Telling: Your prediction of the future outcome is negative due to your distorted way of thinking. You think you know the end game of what will happen without any factual evidence.

E.g., I will never love again.

Overgeneralization: You draw a general conclusion about your ability, performance, or self-worth on the basis of a single incident.

E.g., Nobody likes me

Labeling and Mislabeling: You label others or yourself using terms such as lazy, stupid, loser, fat, jerk, by stating them as though they are facts. This is an extreme form of overgeneralization.

E.g., I am just so fat and lazy, and he is a jerk.

Magnification or Minimization: Things are either blown out of proportion, or you deny something is a problem when it actually is.

E.g., It is not a big deal (when it really is to you) and, It is AWFUL that he said that!

Mental Filter: You single out a negative aspect in a given situation and dwelling exclusively on it, thereby perceiving the whole situation as negative.

E.g., My big nose makes me look so unattractive.

Personalization: Your think things are about you, and when you do, your interpretations are distorted, i.e., If someone is negative or angry, you take responsibility for such things that are outside your control even when there is no basis for doing so.

E.g., My child is depressed, and it is my fault.

Should Statements: A pre-condition on how you and others "should" be such as having judgmental and unforgiving expectations that use "musts" and "shoulds."

E.g., I should not be so angry about this." "He should know this already!"

Can you relate to any of the above examples? Does any of them look familiar to you? Can you spot an underlying trend of distorted thinking patterns that may be contributing to your problem?

Using the examples above, I urge you to go on to identify your cognitive distortion. If you are going through the process of identifying your distorted thoughts with a therapist, you may be asked to pay attention to your physical, emotional, and behavioral responses in different situations.

Steps to Identifying Cognitive Distortions

If you want to identify cognitive distortions in your negative automatic thoughts due to your emotions or feelings from a given situation, ensure to do the following:

- Name the feeling, e.g., Ask yourself, "What am I feeling? And respond, "I am feeling anxious and sad."
- Validate the feeling, e.g., Put your hand over your heart and say "anxious," "sad," and breathe into the feeling of being anxious and sad. Observe where you felt these feelings in your body, focus on that part of your body, and send warm breath to it like you would a child who feels sad.
- <u>Find the thoughts (cognitive distortions) under the feeling by asking yourself:</u>

"What are the thoughts that trigger these feelings?"

E.g., Last night, I was at a work party where I drank too much. When I talked to people at the party, I think I made a fool of myself, and probably said or did something I should not have. Everyone now thinks I am completely screwed up. I would have no more friends, and my boss will fire me; I cannot show up at work tomorrow. I am so mortified that I feel like disappearing. I am such a fat pig.

Some of the thoughts are, "I made a fool of myself, and everyone thinks I am completely screwed up, no one will want to be my friend, I am getting fired, I am a fat pig." These are examples of cognitive distortions. Let's see why below.

- Name the cognitive distortion:

    Should Statements: I should never look out of control.

    Jumping to Conclusions: No one will want to be my friend. I am getting fired.

Labeling and Mislabeling: I am a fat pig

Step 4: Cognitive Restructuring or Challenging Your Negative Automatic Thoughts

Cognitive restructuring or challenging negative automatic thoughts is a mainstay of CBT. It describes the process by which people are trained to change how they think by the examination of their thoughts for bias or inaccuracy and replacing them with more balanced thoughts.

After identifying your cognitive distortions, your therapist will encourage you to question yourself on if your perspective of a situation is based on facts or on an inaccurate view of what is going on. This will help you to challenge them by responding reasonably at each step.

A number of CBT techniques are available in challenging negative thoughts and responding reasonably to them. I will, however, discuss some of the most common ones below:

- Traditional disputation. This method involves the examination of the evidence for and against a thought. People often find reasons why a thought is true but may need assistance in considering why a particular thought may not be 100% true at all times. Once evidence for and against an automatic thought has been generated, either you or at the behest of your therapist would be required to write a balanced thought, taking into account all of the evidence generated.

- Court-trial style disputation. Some people find it helpful when they view the disputation process using the court-trial style. In this method, you will function as the defense attorney, prosecutor, jury, and judge all at once. The automatic thought is placed 'in the dock,' and as the defense attorney, you will argue why the thought is true, and as the prosecutor, why it is false. As the jury, you weigh the evidence, and as the judge, you read the verdict, taking into account all of the evidence.

- Compassionate cognitive restructuring. This method examines the negative thought through a compassionate lens by considering the compassionate perspective of what you would say to others in a similar situation as well as what a compassionate person would say to you.

Finding the Objective Truth About the Thoughts

Using the technique above and the example cited under *Steps to Identifying Cognitive Distortions*, I will demonstrate how to challenge your thoughts and respond rationally.

- What is absolutely true for the cognitive distortions identified?

    What is absolutely true is that I drank a lot and that I am mortified and feel like disappearing.

- How do you know this is true?

    Because I said things I would not have said if I was not drinking.

- Are there any thoughts here that might be untrue?

It might be untrue I made a fool out of myself. It might be untrue I did or said something I should not have. It might be untrue everyone thinks I screwed up. It might be untrue I would not have any more friends.

- How do you know these thoughts might be untrue?

Because I am not a mind reader, and I cannot decipher what everyone thinks.

- What is the more balanced truth here?

The truth is that I am not the first person to have gotten drunk at an office party. As a matter of fact, many people were drinking, and some drank a lot. I doubt many people noticed what I said or did. In functions like this, most people are usually very anxious about what others think of them that I imagine only a few people waste their time obsessing over what I did or did not say. Besides, if one night of being drunk makes me lose my friends, I will know they were not real friends anyway.

You can then go ahead to respond reasonably to each type of cognitive distortions we identified. Using the sample questions and answers from step 2, *Identifying Core Beliefs About the Problems*, let's now also respond reasonably to the distortions in thoughts (assuming you have already applied the techniques above to find the objective truth as already demonstrated).

Initial Responses (Automatic Thoughts)	Reasonable Responses
She's a slob!	To be frank, she's very neat in areas that are important to her, such as her looks.
My friends may see how messy her room is when they come over	Even if they do, several mothers have daughters whose room might be sloppy but yet worthwhile.
They will think I am an inadequate mother	They might just think I am as fallible as they are.
I will feel worthless if my friends disapprove of me = CORE BELIEF!	I don't have to be perfect or have the approval of anyone to be happy and to feel worthwhile. Since no one is perfect, I would rather decide to feel worthwhile for myself.

Going through the process above will help you become rational in reframing not only your negative automatic thoughts but also your negative core beliefs.

Making the Restructured Thoughts Habitual

It is often helpful when you overlearn the habit of identifying automatic thoughts and restructuring your automatic negative thinking. Once you have sufficiently practiced the art of journaling your thoughts using a thought record, it is worthwhile to go through the disputation practice in your head. Your therapist can help you through this process as you do so. Many people often report that doing this soon becomes second-nature to them in noticing automatic thoughts when they pop up – prompting them to ask, among others, "What is the evidence to believe this thought is true?".

An example;

After therapy, Joan learned to monitor her actions and emotional responses. She began by planning the activities that gave her a boost in dealing with the situations she had avoided through fear. She learned to identify when she was biased or extreme in her thinking and became very skilled at analyzing her emotion-driven thoughts by reasoning them out to get things into the right perspective. Her mood after that, noticeably improved, and she was able to tackle long-standing problems.

Step 5: Monitor Your Feelings

Cognitive behavioral therapy places great emphasis on monitoring problems and symptoms. Just like thoughts can be biased, our impressions about the effectiveness of therapy can also be biased. You and/or your therapist can overcome this bias by often measuring the symptoms and problems about whether the therapy is going in the right direction. Regularly monitoring outcomes can help achieve better results.

Symptom monitoring can be as simple as checking in with the feeling again and asking, how are you feeling now?

Still anxious, but a bit relaxed. For now, I can get up and walk away from this. I don't have to stuff something down my mouth to feel better. I can breathe through it, knowing that several of my feelings of anger, guilt, sadness, and shame are not the objective truth, but rather, just self-imposed thoughts.

Symptom monitoring can also mean counting how often something happens, such as counting how often a person with panic experiences panic attacks, or counting how often a person with OCD exhibits one of their compulsions. For anxiety and depression, specific measures might be used to explore the kinds of thoughts experienced by someone.

John came to therapy because he experiences panic attacks. At the beginning of therapy, he was asked by his therapist to keep a record of how many panic attacks he experiences every week. Then each week, they would check for updates on what was happening. Upon completion of treatment, John was pleased not to have experienced any panic attacks in the previous three weeks.

Ultimately, monitoring your feelings, symptoms, or problems aims to check if the goal(s) set in step 1 has been met.

The steps involved in CBT, as discussed above, are the generally accepted method of administering CBT to anyone with a mental or health condition. That being said, conditions such as anxiety and depression, among others, require other specific techniques to be employed as complementary efforts to these steps. The next section of this book would focus on how to use other specific CBT techniques against anxiety, depression, anger, and panic attacks.

See you on the other side!

Exercise

- Based on our discussions in this chapter, use the thought record below to identify your problem situation/ trigger (depression, anxiety, anger or panic attacks related), the emotions or feelings you experienced from the situation, the distorted/ irrational thoughts you had about the situation, the evidence against the distorted thoughts, and your restructured, realistic and more balanced thoughts.

Situation / Trigger	Feelings Emotions – (Rate 0 – 100%) Body sensations	Distorted/ Unhelpful Thoughts / Images	Facts providing evidence against the unhelpful thoughts	Restructured and more balanced, realistic thoughts	Outcome Re-rate emotion
What happened? Where? When? Who with? How?	What emotion did you feel at the time? What else? How intense was it? What did you notice in your body? Where did you feel it?	What went through your mind? What disturbed you? What did those thoughts/ images mean to you, or say about you or the situation? What are you responding to? What would the worst thing about that be, or that could happen?	What facts do you have to validate that the unhelpful thoughts are not true? Is it possible that this is an opinion and not a fact? What did others say about this?	STOP! Take a breath... What would someone else say about this situation? Is there a bigger picture? Is there some other way of seeing it? What advice would you give someone else in a similar situation? Is my reaction proportional to the actual event? Is this really as important as it seems?	What are you feeling now? (0-100%) What else can you do differently that could be more effective? What will be the consequences? What will be most helpful for you or the situation?

Section II

Cognitive Behavioral Therapy Strategies

Chapter 3

CBT for Depression

Understanding Depression

Depression is a low mood that can last for a significant amount of time. The severity of depression varies from a mild depression – which might not prevent you from carrying out your normal activities or seeking enjoyment in life, even though it might be difficult to do, to more severe depression – which can leave you unable to function normally and with feelings of suicide and death. The major component of depression is that the pervasive feeling of sadness continues for weeks or months on end, and not just a passing 'blue mood' for a day or two. Depression (commonly called clinical depression or major depressive disorder) is a feeling that is often accompanied by lack of energy (or feeling "weighed down"), a sense of hopelessness, and having little or no interest in the things that once gave joy and happiness.

Major Depressive Disorder is the leading cause of disability in the US (among ages 15-44), according to the National Institute of Mental Health (NIMH), and it is estimated that about 6.7% of the adult population in the US is affected by Major Depressive Disorder in a given year. According to NIMH (2019), risk factors associated with depression ranges from a family history of mood disorders to trauma, major life changes, other physical diseases (e.g., cancer), or even certain prescription medications.

Symptoms of Depression

As already mentioned, depression does not end after just a day or two — it will continue for weeks on end, causing interference with the person's school, work their relationship with others, as well as their ability to enjoy life and have fun.

The symptoms of depression include most of the signs highlighted below, and are experienced nearly every day over two or more weeks:

- a continuous feeling of sadness or loneliness
- lack of energy or feeling weighed down
- feelings of hopelessness

- sleeping difficulties (too much or too little)
- eating difficulties (too much or too little)
- difficulties with concentration or attention
- complete loss of interest in socializing or fun activities
- feelings of worthlessness and guilt
- and/or thoughts of suicide or death

It should interest you to know that most people who feel depressed do not experience every symptom mentioned above, and the presentation of symptoms also differs in degree and intensity from person to person.

Causes & Diagnosis

Ever wondered what causes depression? Perhaps you have been diagnosed with a major depressive disorder, and that has led you to question why some get depressed, and others don't.

Depression does not discriminate against who it can affect, not by age, race, gender, relationship status, or if a person is rich or poor. Anyone can be affected by depression at any point in their life, and that includes children and adolescents (although sometimes, it is seen more as irritability than a sad mood in teens and children).

No single factor is identified to be responsible for this condition. A combination of factors is likely the cause. For some, there are clear triggers, while for others, it can be difficult to understand why they are depressed. Irrespective of which it is, depression can be a result of genetics, gut bacteria, personality, neurobiological makeup, family history, and psychological, environmental, and social factors. Other factors that may increase the possibility of depression are:

- certain medications
- **critical incidents,** e.g., losses (death of a loved one, end of a relationship, job loss), transitions (retiring, having a baby), or financial problems
- abuse
- serious illness
- substance abuse and;
- the tendency to think negatively

CBT Treatment for Depression

Can depression be successfully treated? Yes, fortunately, **depression is a treatable disorder**. According to NIMH and several research studies conducted over the past six decades, clinical depression can readily be treated with short-term, goal-oriented psychotherapy and modern antidepressant medications. For some people, depending on the severity of their condition, a combination of both would work best. Psychotherapy, which has been scientifically proven to work with depression is one of the most laudable treatments for all types of depression, and the approach it uses include cognitive behavioral therapy, psychodynamic therapy, and interpersonal therapy (Gelenberg et al., 2010). Amongst these approaches, CBT is the most widely recognized and generally accepted method being practiced in the modern world.

When it comes to CBT, several techniques, tools, and interventions are available at your disposal. Some of these techniques are best-suited in a therapist-patient setting, while for others, they lend themselves quite well to an individual or 'self-help' situation.

CBT techniques can likewise be used in tandem or individually. It all depends on the setting, the issue, or the circumstance, as well as the person seeking help. That is one cool thing with CBT techniques – there is no one-size-fits-all, or 'cookie-cutter' way to use them.

The techniques I am going to discuss here all have one thing in common – they are built upon the foundations of CBT, which is identifying maladaptive thinking and making intentional, specific, and strategic behavioral changes to achieve the desired result. There are general CBT techniques (like that discussed in [Chapter 2](), which is the golden standard for all types of conditions), while others are more targeted to specific needs or issues, and these techniques that are more targeted to certain needs (e.g., someone suffering from depression) would be my focus in the following sections.

Before we deep dive into these specific techniques you can start applying right away, it is essential we first discuss some key concepts to give you a solid research-based perspective on how depression works.

What Keeps Depression Going?

Cognitive behavioral therapy is always very interested in figuring out what keeps a problem going. The reason for this is because if we can figure out what keeps a problem going, then we can treat it by distorting its maintenance cycle. To understand what keeps depression going, CBT therapists and researchers proposed two major theories:

- Behavioral model

- Cognitive model

If you have religiously followed the pages of this book, by now, you would have realized that we have virtually touched on all the models above. However, I want to take a different approach to briefly explain these models as it pertains to depression.

Behavioral Theory of Depression

The behavioral theory of depression notes the presence of a strong relationship between the things you do and how you feel. Take, for instance, when you feel good, you are more than likely to partake in activities you enjoy, spend time with people who make you happy, and take on new tasks and adventures that are challenging to you as a person.

The reverse is likewise true, which is you are more than likely to do less when you are depressed, and so, you are left with fewer opportunities to feel pleasure from the activities you enjoy, take on new tasks, and spend time friends and loved ones – the things you need to feel good. This makes it easy to fall into the trap of:

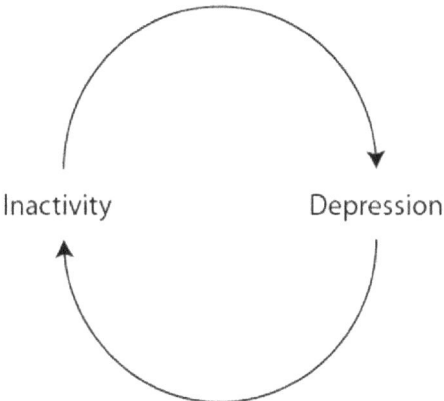

Figure 9: The behavioral model postulates that a lack of rewarding activity results in depression, which then results in further inactivity.

When you are depressed, your motivation works in reverse – you will need to become pleasurably active before you can feel good again. One very effective way of breaking the vicious cycle of depression is to increase your level of pleasant activity *even if you do not feel like it*. This behavioral technique is called Behavioral Activation (BA) or Pleasant Activity Scheduling (PAS), an evidence-based treatment for depression – to be discussed in detail shortly.

Cognitive Theory of Depression

According to the cognitive model, depression is underpinned by negatively biased thinking patterns, i.e., *how you think affects how you feel*. For instance, when you are happy, your thoughts become optimistic, and you can see the bright side of things even when stressful situations occur. But when depressed, your thoughts can become very extreme and very negative, which often makes you interpret situations in negative ways that make you feel bad. Depressing thoughts can be about one's self, the world or other people, and one's future.

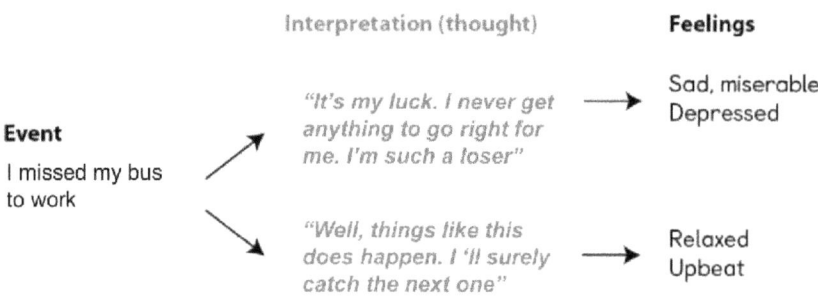

Figure 10: How you interpret events or situations determines how you feel about them.

A cognitive or CBT therapist can help you in identifying unhelpful ways in which you think and will help you in practicing several ways of thinking – one of which might be helping you interpret things in a more balanced way. Two very important techniques used in achieving this are called, Identifying Cognitive Distortions and Cognitive Restructuring. You would agree with me that we discussed extensively on these techniques in Chapter 2, so there won't be a need to revisit them. I advise that you go through Chapter 2 if you are yet to. Another well known cognitive treatment technique for depression, especially in preventing relapse is Mindfulness-Based Cognitive Therapy (MBCT).

CBT Technique for Depression

By the end of this section, I would have discussed four important techniques you can apply right away to overcome depression instantly; the third technique is our next focus.

Behavioral Activation

Behavioral activation (BA), or Pleasant Activity Scheduling is all about making your life pleasurable and meaningful again. A proactive way to break the vicious cycle of depression is to increase your level of activity even if you do not feel like it. To perform behavioral activation effectively, you need to adhere to the following steps:

- Activity monitoring – recording what you do and how you feel daily.
- Reviewing your "activity monitoring" to understand the relationships existing between your activity and your mood.
- Identifying your values to work out what matters to you in life.
- Scheduling and executing worthwhile activities to boost your experiences of pleasure and achievement.
- Solving any problems or barriers to activation – to ensure you stay on course.

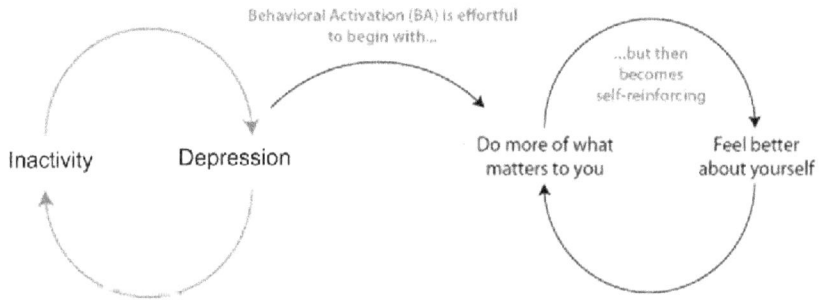

Figure 11

I will walk you through each step highlighted above to get you started with behavioral activation.

Step 1: Activity monitoring

Activity monitoring is the first step in behavioral activation therapy, which aims to monitor your activity and mood for a better understanding of how your depression works.

An activity monitoring worksheet can be used to record what you do for every hour of the day and for a week. Ensure you record everything on this worksheet, even the activities that do not seem important to you. Also, for each time slot, rate your mood on a scale of 1 to 5 – 1 represents feeling very depressed, and 5 represents feeling very good. The goal is to work out how your mood changes as you undertake different activities.

	Monday	Tuesday	Wednesday	Sunday	Mood
06:00 – 07:00	Sleeping	Went Shopping	Facebook	Watched Tv	2
07:00 – 08:00					
08:00 – 09:00					
09:00 – 10:00					
10:00 – 11:00					
11:00 – 12:00					
12:00 – 13:00					

Key

Mood

1 = Very Depressed
2 = Mildly Depressed
3 = Neutral
4 = Fairly Good
5 = Very Good

Exercise 1

1. Using the template above, make a note of every activity you do for each hour of the day for 7 days a week. This can be recorded in a journal or on a note-taking app on your phone.

Step 2: Review your activity monitoring

After monitoring your activity for a week, use your activity monitoring record to spot patterns between your activity and your mood. Look at your completed activity monitoring worksheet and ask yourself the following questions:

- Which activities are associated with your highest mood? When your mood was highest, what were you doing?
- Which activities are associated with your lowest mood? When your mood was lowest, what were you doing?
- What did you observe about the relationship that existed between your mood and how active you were?
- Were there days you did not leave the house? On those days, what was your mood like?
- On the days you were most active, what was your mood like?

Exercise 2

1. Upon answering the questions above, make a list of the activities that made you feel good, and made you feel bad. This list will be used in step 4.

Activities That Made Me Feel Good	Activities That Made Me Feel Bad
1	1
2	2

Step 3: Identify your values

Our values are a reflection of what we hold dear in life. They are what you deeply care about and consider to be important. Our values also reflect how we engage with ourselves, with the those around us, and with the world. Values differ from goals in that goals are achievable. For example, you might hold the value of *being a good parent* very dear to you, which may require an effort of a lifetime, while having a specific goal of *getting your children to school on time*.

Below are examples of values held dear by some people. There might be values you feel that are essential, and others that do not mean much to you. There are no right or wrong answers. Using the descriptions below, think of what makes a meaningful life that you could value.

Value	Description
Family	What kind of relationship do you wish to have with your family? What type of /father / brother / mother /sister/ uncle/ aunt / nephew/ niece/ do you wish to be? How do you wish to be in these relationships?
Marriage / couple / intimacy	What kind of husband/wife/partner do you wish to be? What type of relationship do you wish to be a part of? What type of partnership do you wish to build? What kind of person do you wish to be in a relationship?
Parenting	What type of parent do you wish to be? What qualities do you wish your children see in you? What kind of relationship do you wish to build with your children?
Friendships / social life	What type of friend do you wish to be? What type of friendships is important for you to cultivate? How would you prefer to behave toward your friends? What kind of social life is important to you?
Career /	What kind of work do you find

employment	valuable to you? What are the qualities you wish to bring as an employee? What kind of work relationships would you rather build?
Education / personal growth / development	How would you want to grow as a person? What kind of skills would you want to develop? What matters to you about education and learning? What would you like to know more about?
Recreation/ fun / leisure	How would you like to enjoy yourself? What relaxes you? When are you most playful?
Spirituality	What kind of relationship do you want with God/nature / the Earth?
Citizenship / environment / community	What kind of environment do you want to be a part of? How do you want to contribute to your community? What kind of citizen would you like to be?
Health / physical wellbeing	What kind of values do you have regarding your physical wellbeing? How important to you is your health? How do you want to look after yourself?

Exercise 3

1. Using the examples provided above, take some time thinking about your values – which do you find important to you? How successful have you lived your life in the past month per your values? Use the table below to guide your thought process as you document your response in your journal and feel free to add more values not captured in the table.

Value	Description of your values	Importance How important is this value to you? (Rate 1-5)	Success How successful have you lived per this value in the past month? (Rate 1–5)
Family			
Marriage / couple / intimacy			
Parenting			
Friendships / social life			
Career / employment			
Education / personal growth / development			
Recreation/ fun / leisure			
Spirituality			
Citizenship / environment / community			

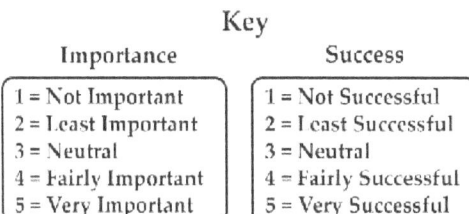

Step 4: Scheduling and executing worthwhile activities

The next step of behavioral activation is to become active. By now, you know it is important to increase your activity level even if you do not feel like it. To kick-start the planning of your activity and sticking to it, write down a selection of likely activities in your journal.

Great places to get some activation targets for your activity plan are:

- **From your activity monitoring exercise:** Which activities worked best at improving your mood from step 2 exercise?
- **From your values assessment exercise:** Which values matter most to you? What activities could you do that may line up with your values? If for example, family is one of the things you value

most, perhaps as an activity, you could plan to spend quality time with them.
- **Ensure you do the basics:** Be sure to include targets such as daily brushing of your teeth, doing laundry weekly, cooking meals, shopping, and some socializing activities.
- **Use an activity menu:** Using a list of the activities that helped other people, pick some you think would lift your mood. You can take a cue from the sample activity menu below.

> **Activity Menu**
> Do some exercise
> Meet a friend for coffee
> Cook a meal for someone
> Clean the house
> Take a bath
> Listen to music you like
> Do something nice for someone

Exercise 4

1. After writing down a selected list of possible activities, it is time to create an activity hierarchy. This will help you select the best activities to start with. To create your activity hierarchy, write down the list of the possible activities, and rank

them per how difficult you feel they will be to accomplish (1 = not difficult, 5 = very difficult).

See sample below

Activity	Difficulty (Rate 1-5)
Go to an exercise class once this week	5
Get out of bed by 8 am every day	4
Go for a haircut	3
Repair the kitchen shelf	2

2. Schedule by writing down some activities for the next week by selecting some activities that have low difficulty ratings. It is important that you are specific about:

- **What** the activity is
- **When** you will do it
- **Where** you will do it
- **Who** you might do it with

See sample below

Activity (What?)	Details (When? Where? Who?)	Outcome & Rate Mood (Rate mood 1-5)
Go to an exercise class	Tuesday at 6 pm	Completed - 5
Get out of bed	By 8 am every day	5 out of 7 days - 2
Go for a haircut	Thursday lunchtime, barber near home	Completed - 4
Repair the kitchen shelf	Monday morning, at home	Completed - 3

Key

Mood

1 = Very Depressed
2 = Mildly Depressed
3 = Neutral
4 = Fairly Good
5 = Very Good

After planning the activities in advance for a week, the next step is to put them into action. Good luck!

Step 5: Solving any problems or barriers to activation

- **Do not start too hard:** Life is not a sprint but a marathon. Overall, your activity level has to be greater than your depression level; however, it has to be realistically achievable.
- **Break down activities into smaller steps:** Let's assume you identified the value of being independent, but you are living with your parents. Some helpful steps you can take toward your value might be doing some financial

budgeting and planning to work out a move into your own place.
- **Reward yourself:** Make the effort in acknowledging when you completed an activity and not just rushing onto the next target. Some people use a 'check off' for activities that have been completed as an acknowledgment that it has been done. What would a fair reward be if all activities were completed? Think of a way you can treat yourself if you completed half or all of your planned activities.
- **Always remind yourself why you are doing this:** Thoughts like *"when I feel better I'll do it"* are insidious, and depression through this can creep back in. Ofter remind yourself that it is important to be active *even if you do not feel like it* and that one of the most effective treatments for depression is through behavioral activation.

Mindfulness

Mindfulness-based cognitive therapy (MBCT) is a type of therapy birthed from the union of cognitive therapy and meditative principles. The marriage of these ideas resulted in a potent therapeutic tool **used by therapists** in helping people experience a unique kind of relationship with their thoughts and minds.

Two experiments conducted to test the effectiveness of MBCT on depression showed that the relapse rates for this disorder decreased (Teasdale et al., 2000; Kuyken et al., 2008), while a more recent study in patients from several age groups demonstrated the applicability of MBCT in treating different illnesses such as depression, and anxiety (Haydicky, Carly, Wiener, & Ducharme, 2015; Kishita, Takei, & Stewart, 2016; Schroevers, Tovote, Snippe, & Fleer, 2016). Although mindfulness is widely used, one area MBCT is thought to have strong evidence in its effectiveness is in the treatment of people who have experienced three or more depressive episodes – thus helpful, especially to prevent relapse in depression (Mental Health Foundation).

There are lots of mindfulness techniques and techniques that can help you cope with mental illness such as depression, and they can be practiced with or without the guidance of a therapist. Some of these techniques include:

- Mindful Meditation
- Mindful Observation
- Mindful Listening
- Mindful Breathing
- Mindful Walking
- Guided Meditation
- Self-Compassion Break and;
- Body Scan

In my book, ***How to Stop Overthinking***, I discussed extensively on each of these techniques and how they can be practised effectively.

Vagus Nerve Stimulation Therapy

As you explore your depression during therapy or self-administration, you may also want complementary therapies designed to bring down your overall depression levels and help you achieve emotional balance. One such therapy that has gained wide acceptance and now being practised in the treatment of depression is called **Vagus Nerve Stimulation,** a nerve that wanders from your brain into your body, i.e., from your brainstem linking your neck, thorax (chest), and abdomen (belly).

In this unique treatment approach, a vagus nerve stimulation device is used, which is **administered by gently pressing the device against your neck to stimulate the vagus nerve by sending pulses of electrical signals to this nerve.** The vagus nerve is targeted because of its ability to modulate depression, and it has been demonstrated to be highly effective in treatment-resistant depression.

Other vagus nerve stimulation practices are likewise used as a treatment option for depression. Such practices include:

- Deep and slow breathing
- Sudarshan Kriya Yoga, and;
- Auricular Acupuncture among others

In his book, *The Secrets of Vagus Nerve Stimulation*, Dr. Lee Henton demystifies the complexities of the vagus nerve in the treatment of depression and other conditions such as anxiety. If you are interested in reading further on the subject of Vagus Nerve Stimulation as an alternative/ complementary therapy for depression, then click this link or use this web address https://amzn.to/2Kp4PAK.

Chapter 4

CBT for Anxiety

Understanding Anxiety, Worry, and Fear

According to the National Institute of Mental Health (NIMH), about 19% of US adults and 31% of adolescents (ages 13 to 18) experience anxiety every year. Anxiety is an umbrella term that describes feelings of worry, fear, nervousness, or apprehensiveness – these are all part of our everyday lives. We all get anxious about something at some point in our lives, but simply experiencing the feelings of anxiety does not mean you need to seek professional help or that you suffer from an anxiety disorder. In fact, anxiety is an essential and sometimes helpful warning signal against a dangerous or difficult situation. Without anxiety, we would be unable to anticipate dangers and difficulties and prepare for them. Anxiety becomes a disorder when the symptoms become chronic that it occurs quite too often, goes on for a long time, and interferes with your daily activities and ability to function properly.

Anxiety disorders fall into a set of distinct diagnoses, which is dependent on the severity and symptoms of the anxiety being experienced by a person. Different types of unhealthy thoughts are also associated with different types of anxiety disorder. These disorders include:

- Panic disorder/ Panic Attacks
- Obsessive-compulsive disorder (OCD)/ Intrusive Thoughts
- Phobias (e.g., Agoraphobia, Specific/Simple Phobia, and Social Phobia/Anxiety)
- Generalized anxiety disorder (GAD)
- Social anxiety disorder (SAD)
- Post-traumatic stress disorder (PTSD)

Irrespective of the specific disorder, they often follow a similar pattern, i.e., people who suffer from anxiety tend to react more extremely to unpleasant/ unhelpful thoughts, feelings, and situations and may try managing their reactions by **avoiding triggers**. Sadly, such avoidance behavior only serves to reinforce fears and worries. To manage anxiety, most modern types of therapy tend to address this negative thinking and avoidance behavior.

Symptoms of Anxiety

At some point in time of our lives, we have experienced fleeting symptoms associated with anxiety. Such feelings — such as your heart pounding for no apparent reason, having shortness of breath, experiencing tunnel vision, or dizziness usually pass by as quickly as they come and do not return readily. However, when they do return time after time, that can be a sign the fleeting feelings of anxiety have metamorphosed into an anxiety disorder. People who suffer from anxiety disorder also report the following symptoms:

- Muscle tension
- Physical weakness
- Poor memory
- Sweaty hands
- Fear or confusion
- Inability to relax
- Constant worry
- Upset stomach and;
- Poor concentration

Causes & Diagnosis

Anxiety can be caused by several factors that range from external stimuli, shame, emotional abandonment to experiencing an extreme reaction to something that is potentially anxiety-provoking when first exposed to it. Research is yet to explain why some people experience panic attacks or develop phobias, while others who grow up in the same family with shared experiences do not experience the same. The plausible reason for this is that anxiety disorders, like all mental illness, are caused by a set of complex factors that are not yet fully understood. These factors include childhood development, neurobiology, genetics, psychological factors, personality development, including social and environmental cues.

Like most mental disorders, diagnosing anxiety disorders are best performed by a mental health professional — a specialist trained on the nuances of mental disorder diagnoses (such as a psychiatrist or psychologist).

CBT Treatment for Anxiety

Whether you suffer from panic attacks, obsessive thoughts, constant worries, or an incapacitating phobia, it is important to know you do not have to live with anxiety and fear.

Anxiety disorders can be readily treated through a mix of psychotherapy and anti-anxiety medications. Most people taking medications for anxiety disorders do take them on a need-to-use basis, for the specific situation that causes the anxiety reaction.

In some cases, medications play a role in the treatment of **anxiety disorders**. But for most people, therapy alone is the most viable treatment option. The reason for this is that therapy, unlike medication, treats more than just the symptoms of the problem. Therapy can help you to uncover the root cause of your worries and fears, help you learn how to relax, help you look at situations differently in new, less frightening ways, and can help you in developing better coping and problem-solving skills. Therapy provides you with the tools to overcome anxiety and teaches you how to use them both in the present and in the future.

Several therapeutic techniques have been designed in treating anxiety, evolving from psychoanalytic approaches to the most widely used and recognized therapy called cognitive behavioral therapy.

Many studies have shown that CBT, as the golden standard, is very effective in the treatment of anxiety (1).

CBT focuses on:

- Changing unhealthy/ negative thinking that contributes to your anxiety (using cognitive therapy), and;

- Changing your behavior patterns (using behavior therapy) to help you manage the factors that contribute to your anxiety so that you experience less anxiety over time.

Just like depression, several CBT techniques have been developed to address anxiety. However, the leading techniques proven to be very effective against anxiety are:

- Identifying cognitive distortions and cognitive restructuring
- Exposure therapy and;
- Relaxation training such as deep breathing exercises, progressive muscle relaxation, and mindfulness

Although the particular type of anxiety disorder requires the intervention or technique to be individualized or tailored, the anxiety treatments highlighted above, nonetheless, have shown effectiveness for most people with anxiety disorders.

As we deep dive into the aforementioned techniques, kindly refer to Chapter 2 for an in-depth discussion on; identifying cognitive distortions and cognitive restructuring – this is a golden standard for all types of conditions.

Exposure Therapy

It is generally the case that severe anxiety reflects more of worry over the anxiety itself as opposed to the problem underneath.

The Greek philosopher Epictetus said:

"Man is not worried by real problems so much as by his imagined anxieties about real problems." —**Epictetus**

For example, a person with a phobia for public speaking is typically terrified to look like a fool before an audience due to his/her anxiety symptoms (e.g., throwing-up, passing-out, stuttering, sweating, etc.).

Therefore, the real problem is not the fear of public speaking per se, but rather, it is the anticipation of the associated anxiety that causes fear. It is only by confronting such anxiety that people often experience relief. This technique of confronting your anxiety is called **Exposure Therapy** – a behavior-type therapy.

Exposure therapy is a type of CBT technique that is generally considered the best psychological approach in treating anxiety disorders **such as panic disorder, phobia, OCD, PTSD, and SAD**. The primary premise behind exposure therapy is that if you are afraid of something, the best way to conquer it is by going at it head-on (facing your fears). The problem with avoiding your fears is that you will never have the opportunity to overcome them. In fact, avoiding your fears makes them even stronger.

When you are exposed to the source of your anxieties, and nothing terrible happens, the anxiety reduces. This does not mean you should throw yourself (if, for instance, you have a fear of spiders) into a room of tarantulas (a type of spider species) and lock the door, although some have had success with this—it is called "flooding." However, I don't recommend you do this except you really know what you are doing. Instead, you will gradually work your way up to the stimuli you fear.

During exposure therapy, a therapist will slowly introduce you to objects or situations that trigger anxiety or situations you fear. The idea is that when exposed repeatedly, you will feel an increasing sense of control over the situation, thus diminishing your anxiety – this process is called systematic desensitization, and it involves three important parts:

Learning relaxation skills. Your therapist will first teach you a technique for relaxation (this I will show you subsequently), such as deep breathing, progressive muscle relaxation, or mindfulness, which you will have to practice during therapy and at home. Once you start confronting your fears, this relaxation technique will be used to reduce your bodily or physical anxiety response (such as hyperventilating and trembling) and encourage relaxation.

Creating a step-by-step list. Next, you will create a list of about 10 to 20 situations you are scared of, forming a hierarchy that progresses toward your final goal, and ranking them in terms of their intensity, i.e., from the least anxiety-provoking situation to what causes you the most anxiety. For instance, if your final goal is overcoming your fear of flying, you will start the list with "looking at flying airplanes," to "driving with a loved one to the airport," and ending the list with "taking an actual flight with a trusted companion by your side." Each step would be as specific as possible, with a clear and measurable objective.

Exposure (working through the steps). Your therapist will guide you as you work through the list. The goal is to stay put in each scary situation until your fears have subsided. That way, you will learn that you won't be hurt by the feelings of anxiety, thus making them go away. Every time you experience the anxiety becoming too intense, you will turn on the relaxation technique you learned. Once relaxed again, you can then revert your attention to the scary situation. In this way, you will work through each step until you can complete each one without the feeling of being overly distressed.

The exposure to your anxiety-provoking stimuli is usually done in one of three ways in which a therapist can help you in determining the best fit for your situation. The most common are:

- Imaginary exposure: You will be instructed to imagine the feared object or situation vividly. For example, someone who suffers from PTSD might be required to recollect and paint a picture of his/her traumatic experience to help reduce the feelings of fear.

- In-vivo exposure: You will be required to directly face a feared object or situation in real life. For example, someone with a phobia of snakes might be directed to handle a snake, or someone with social anxiety condition might be directed to give a speech before an audience.

- Interoceptive exposure: You might be deliberately exposed to bodily or physical sensations that are harmless, but yet feared. For example, someone with panic attacks might be directed to run to make his/her heart speed up, and encouraged to maintain contact with the feared sensations – therefore, learning that this sensation is not harmful.

Each of these forms of exposure therapy work for a specific type of anxiety disorder. Thus, in explaining how exposure therapy works using the above, I would streamline the discussion to address specifically how one or more of the above forms can be used to stop panic attacks in its tracks. But before I delve into this, it is important I discuss why success with exposure therapy is not always guaranteed even though it is very effective. Depending on the anxiety disorder being treated, between 10% and 30% of people fail to respond to exposure therapy (Craske, M. G., 1998. *Anxiety disorders: Psychological approaches to theory and treatment*). While about two-thirds of people follow through with the treatment program to completion, some complete the treatment only to have their fear return afterward. The reason for the failed treatment is often caused by their unwillingness to experience the intense distress associated with an exposure exercise. Also, and perhaps more importantly, many people have not fully grasped the rationale behind exposure-based treatments, thereby making it difficult for them to stick with the treatment when things get tough.

Practicing Exposure Therapy More Effectively

A recent study into the theory of inhibitory learning sheds some light on why some people fail to respond to exposure therapy. As briefly as I can, I will discuss the theory that underpins exposure therapy and review some recent findings from research that can help you practice exposure therapy more effectively to increase its chances of success.

At this point, you have one choice:

- Skip straight to learn and apply the techniques of exposure therapy against panic attacks.
- Read on to learn about the relevant theory first and then learn how these insights can be put into practice to increase the success rate of exposure therapy and making it more effective.

Habituation: The Backbone of Exposure Therapy

Exposure-based treatments ride on a natural process called habituation. Habituation is when a person, after repeated exposure, stops paying attention or responding to a stimulus, such as an object, thought, person, place, or action.

Examples of habituation can be seen in our everyday life. For instance, when you first moved into a new neighborhood, you may be aggravated by the constant noise of a busy highway running near your house. However, with each day passing by, the noise from the highway fades into the background until you can no longer notice it. In this example, you have become habituated to the sound of the highway.

Another example, but this time, with fear habituation as the goal. In conducting exposure therapy for fear of an object, person, situation, thought, or place, the exposure trial is performed continuously until the person has habituated to a point where he/ she reports a significant reduction in fear. For example, if a person with a phobia of spiders reports a fear rating of 8/10 and then afterward, he/ she is presented with a spider, the therapist would wait until the rating of 4/10 or less is reported before terminating the exposure trial. Thus, exposure-based behavior therapies work when habituation to things that are feared is promoted by creating the opportunity to unlearn the associations of dangerous or threatening situations.

Although the above holds as mentioned for habituation, its account, however, of exposure therapy is faulted in some aspects and raises both empirical and pragmatic concerns, the most important of these is that:

- During therapy sessions, habituation does not seem to be necessary for longer-term reduction of fear (Craske, M. G., Kircanski, K., Zelikowsky, M., Mystkowski, J., Chowdhury, N., & Baker, A., 2008. *Optimizing inhibitory learning during exposure therapy. Behaviour Research and Therapy, 46(1), 5-27*). What this means is that even those who do not report reduced fear ratings during an exposure exercise can go on to experience a significant reduction in fear later on. Thus, extinction of fear can happen even if habituation has not happened.

- Stressing the importance of fear reduction during exposure exercise means anxiety is inherently bad and that treatment can only be successful when one is anxiety-free. The implication of this is that people are made to being afraid of fear, causing them to view unexpected but normal surges of fear as signs of failure (Jacoby, R. J., & Abramowitz, J. S., 2016. *Inhibitory learning approaches to exposure therapy: A critical review and translation to obsessive-compulsive disorder. Clinical Psychology Review, 49, 28-40*). A type of CBT, Acceptance, and Commitment Therapy (ACT), has thrown this position into sharp relief.

Are you still surprised about the doubts cast on the overall effectiveness of habituation per exposure exercise? Not to worry because, by the time I am done discussing inhibitory learning theory, which is our next focus, you will better understand why habituation does not seem to be all too important for exposure therapy to be effective.

Inhibitory Learning: A Framework for Understanding Exposure

The theory of inhibitory learning was developed to shed light on the process of fear extinction. Fear extinction is the type of learning that happens during exposure therapy when a person confronts his/ her fear-inducing stimulus without experiencing the terrible effects of the fear stimulus. As a result:

- Their expectancies are modified in that they no longer expect the fear-inducing stimulus to result in the terrible consequences of the fear stimulus. For example, a person with a phobia of spiders who handles spiders repeatedly no longer expects spiders to jump at him/ her. Or the person with panic disorder who exposes himself repeatedly to feelings of breathlessness no longer expects to feel that body sensation when he/she passes out.

- Their behavior is modified in that they approach their fear-inducing stimulus rather than avoid it. For example, a person who completes exposure therapy for social anxiety will no longer dread going for social events and consequently feeling able to be at gatherings with other people in several contexts. And the person with OCD will no longer avoid sharp objects that normally triggered their obsessive thoughts.

Also, the idea behind the inhibitory theory is that the original threat you learned during fear acquisition from an object, person, situation, thought, or place is not replaced or erased by the new learning after you undergo exposure therapy to confront your fears. Instead, the original threat from the object or situation becomes an ambiguous stimulus that lives both in your memory and competes for its retrieval (retrieval competition). This explains why fear can easily return for some people who completed the exposure treatment, while for others, they entirely fail to respond to treatment. Inhibitory learning argues that the reason for this is because the original threat that indicates danger is winning the retrieval competition at that moment and that the new learning that does not indicate danger is not winning, therefore it is not inhibiting the old and original threat.

Figure 12: How fear is learned (fear acquisition)

Inhibitory learning also **explains why habituation does not seem all too important for exposure therapy to be** effective. This reason for this is not far fetched other than it is the learning that determines the new expectancies and behavior. Inhibitory learning argues that habituation can be good for a person and can be linked with fear extinction, however, what the person learns about the relationship between the fear-inducing stimulus, the terrible effects of the fear stimulus, and about their fear itself, is more important.

What to do to make Exposure Therapy More Effective

In this section, I would discuss some approaches you can take either as a therapist or as an individual to prevent a relapse in treatment and to increase the chances of the new learning winning the retrieval competition, and thus, increasing the chances of success with exposure therapy.

Removal of Safety Signals

It is common to engage in safety behaviors (actions intended to keep us safe or prevent a catastrophe) when we are afraid. However, engaging in safety behaviors, though potentially helpful, can prevent new learning from occurring. For instance, if you have a dog phobia and you employ the safety behavior of being calm when near a dog, you might conclude that: *"It was only OK that time because I remained calm"* instead of a more helpful conclusion: *"Maybe I can be safe around dogs."*

The best advice, in general, is that opportunities for new learning during exposure therapy and the chances of the new learning winning the retrieval competition are more effective when you drop all safety behaviors as fast as possible.

Also, during the exposure trial, double-check that you are not engaging in avoidance by asking *"Is there anything right now I am doing to stop the catastrophe from happening?"*, *"Am I doing anything presently to cope with how I am feeling?"*. Engaging in avoidance prevents the new learning from inhibiting the old and original threat, thus preventing you from achieving success with exposure therapy.

Multiple Contexts

You might have successfully extinguished a fear in a context, such as a therapist's office, just for the fear to reinforce itself in another context when the phobic stimulus is encountered. For example, you suffer from panic attacks but manage to engage in a range of interoceptive exposure exercises with a therapist; however, you find the same exercises challenging while attempting them at home. According to inhibitory learning theory — you might have developed some new learning, but if a fear returns, then the new learning has not won the retrieval competition at that present time.

The solution to this is making more new learning which is more salient, and more easily retrievable, such as:

- Practicing exposure in many contexts.
- Getting out of the therapy room to practice exposure.
- Setting homework (self-practice) tasks and motivating yourself on why you need to complete them.
- Engaging in imaginary, in-vivo, and interoceptive exposures in several places as possible (work, at home, out and about) and at several times of the day / week / year.

Retrieval Cues

The goal of retrieval cues is finding ways to remind you of what you learned during exposure therapy without having to use it as a safety signal. Carrying cues such as a wrist-band to serve as a reminder of prior learning has been demonstrated as helping to convey the beneficial effects of exposure therapy – this helps you to retrieve the new learning when the old and original threat attempts to inhibit the new learning from winning the retrieval competition. Retrieval cues, however, should be used sparingly and as a relapse-prevention skill (keeping alive the hard-won knowledge).

Now that we have discussed and potentially removed any barriers to successfully implementing the exposure therapy, subsequent sections would focus on how to use the exposure therapy technique to stop panic attacks. But before then, let's talk about relaxation training since it is a prerequisite when confronting your fears to help lower your bodily anxiety response (e.g., trembling).

Relaxation Training

Relaxation training is a technique you can use to initiate a calming response within your body. This technique can help people who suffer from a range of mental health conditions, such as anxiety, depression, panic disorder, OCD, and anger, and can it be practised with or without the guidance of a therapist. Although everyone has his/ her own preferences that they find work best for them, however, three of the most commonly used and effective skills for relaxation are deep breathing, progressive muscle relaxation (PMR), and mindfulness. For this section, I would focus on deep breathing and PMR. If you want further guidance on how to practice mindfulness, refer to the mindfulness section of this book.

Deep breathing (diaphragmatic breathing): This technique requires you to take conscious control of your breath. You will learn how to breathe slowly, using your diagram to initiate your body's relaxation response. Although there are many variations to practicing this technique, I will, however, share one easy-to-use method as given below.

Instructions: Deep Breathing

1. Sit comfortably in your chair, and place your hand on your stomach to help you feel the movement of your diaphragm as you breathe.
2. Through your nose, take a deep breath. Breathe in slowly for about 5 seconds.
3. Hold your breath for another 5 seconds. You can do less time if you feel uncomfortable.

4. Slowly release the air for another 5 seconds. You can also do this by puckering your lips while pretending you are blowing through a straw (actually, it can be quite helpful when using a straw for practice).
5. Repeat this process 3 times a day for about 5 minutes, preferably. The more you engage in this practice, the more effective deep breathing will come through for you when you need it.

Deep breathing can be very valuable in the present moment, especially when confronting an anxiety-producing situation or object, or in general, as a way to reduce overall stress. I advise that you practise deep breathing each day even if you are feeling fine—the effects can be long-lasting.

Progressive Muscle Relaxation (PMR): Unlike deep breathing, PMR requires a bit more effort, and it is shown to reduce feelings of stress and anxiety significantly. Although this exercise provides an instant feeling of relaxation, it is, however, best you practice this technique frequently. With experience, you will be able to recognize when you are experiencing tension, and you will possess the skills to help you relax during anxiety or stress-provoking situations. During

PMR exercise, each muscle will be slowly tensed and then relaxed, but not to the point of strain. If you have an injury or pain around your muscles, you can skip the affected area. PMR requires that you pay close attention to the feeling of releasing tension in each of the muscles and the feeling of relaxation that it produces.

Below is the script to get you started in practising PMR:

Lie down or sit back in a comfortable position, and shut your eyes (if you are comfortable with it).

Start by taking a deep breath, notice the feeling of air filling up your lungs, and hold your breath for some seconds.

(brief pause)

Slowly release your breath and allow the tension to leave your body.

Take another deep breath and hold it.
(brief pause)

Again, release the air slowly.

Now even slower, take in another breath, fill up your lungs and hold the air.
(brief pause)

Slowly release your breath and picture the feeling of tension leaving your body.

Now, direct your attention to your feet. Tense your feet by curling your toes, and your foot's arch. Maintain the tension and notice how it feels.

(5 second pause)

Release the tension in your foot, and notice the new feeling of relaxation.

Next, focus on your lower leg, and begin to tense the muscles in your calves. Hold unto them tightly, paying attention to the feeling of tension.

(5 second pause)

Let go of the tension from your lower legs, and again, notice the feeling of relaxation. Continue to take deep breaths.

Next, tense the muscles of your upper leg and pelvis. This can be done by squeezing your thighs tightly together. Ensure sure you feel tenseness without going to the point of strain.

(5 second pause)

Release and feel the tension as it leaves your muscles.

Next, tense your stomach and chest. This can be done by sucking in your stomach. Squeeze harder and hold the tension a little longer.

(5 second pause)

Let go of the tension, and allow your body to go limp. Notice the feeling of relaxation.

Continue to take deep breaths by breathing slowly. Notice the air fill in your lungs, and hold it.

(brief pause)

Slowly release the air, and feel it leaving your lungs.

Next, tense the muscles in your back. This is done by bringing your shoulders together behind you and holding them tightly. Keep holding them as you tense them as hard as possible without straining.

(5 second pause)

Let go of the tension from your back. Feel the tension as it slowly leaves your body and the new feeling of relaxation. Observe as your body feels different when you allow it to relax.

Next, tense your arms all the way up from your hands to your shoulders, make a fist, and squeeze all the way up your arm. Hold it.

(5 second pause)

Let go of the tension from your arms and shoulders, and notice how your fingers, arms, hands, and shoulders feel relaxed. Also, notice the limp feeling and ease in your arms.

Next, go up to your neck and head, and tense your face and neck by distorting the muscles surrounding your eyes and mouth.

(5 second pause)

Let go of the tension, and notice the new feeling of relaxation.

Lastly, tense your entire body – your feet, legs, stomach, chest, arms, neck, and head. Tense a little harder without straining and hold the tension.

(5 second pause)

Let go of the tension, and allow your entire body to go limp. Pay close attention to the feeling of relaxation, and notice the difference from the feeling of tension.

Start waking your body up by moving your muscles slowly. Adjust your arms and legs.

Stretch your muscles, opening your eyes in the process, or when you are ready.

Complementary Therapy for Anxiety

As you begin to explore your anxiety disorder in therapy or through self-administration, you may also feel the need to experiment with complementary therapies that can bring your overall anxiety and stress levels to the barest minimum and help you achieve emotional balance. Just like depression, **Vagus Nerve Stimulation** is one such therapy with increasing popularity that has gained wide acceptance in the treatment of anxiety. Although this approach is typically used in treatment-resistant depression, studies have gone to demonstrate its effectiveness for treatment-resistant anxiety disorders (George, Ward, & Ninan, 2008). Also, studies where the vagus nerve stimulation was used in treating depression, reported significant reductions in anxiety symptoms (Chavel, Westerveld, & Spencer, 2003; Rush, George, & Sackeim et al., 2000).

Dr. Lee Henton, in his book, *The Secrets of Vagus Nerve Stimulation*, sheds more light on how the vagus nerve works and its effectiveness as a therapeutic approach in the treatment of anxiety. If you are interested in reading further on the subject of Vagus Nerve Stimulation as an alternative/ complementary therapy for anxiety, then click this link or use this web address https://amzn.to/2Kp4PAK.

Panic Attacks

A panic attack is a sudden surge of intense fear or discomfort, which feels as though it appeared out of the blue, reaching a peak within minutes (5 to 30 minutes). Panic attacks often involve the feelings of having at least four of the following symptoms:

- Palpitations, accelerated heart rate or pounding heart
- Shaking or trembling
- Sensations of smothering or shortness of breath
- Feeling of choking
- Sweating
- Discomfort or chest pain
- Dizzy feeling, faint or lightheaded
- Heat sensations or chills
- Abdominal distress or nausea
- Tingling or numbness sensations
- Fear of dying
- Feelings of unreality (derealization) or feelings of being detached from oneself (depersonalization) and;
- Fear of going crazy or losing control

Panic attacks are followed by catastrophic thinkings that something bad or terrible is happening or about to happen. Although panic attacks are not dangerous, they, however, do feel terrifying. Some people might experience a one-off panic attack once in a life-time without experiencing another, while some people would go on to experience multiple and constant panic attacks. People who worry about their panic and take steps in preventing the possibility of having another panic attack episode are said to be suffering from panic disorder.

What Causes Panic Attacks?

The cause of panic attacks is not clear, however, no single cause can be attributed to it. Some of the factors that could increase your chances of experiencing panic attacks and panic disorder include:

- **Strong biological reactions to stress:** Some people's bodies respond more to event-producing stress and produce more stress hormones such as cortisol and adrenaline.
- **Anxiety sensitivity:** Some people have high sensitivity compared to others to the feelings in their bodies. More than likely, they tend to notice them and misinterpret them as being dangerous.
- **Other psychological problems:** People that suffer from a wide range of psychological problems mostly experience panic attacks. For example,

people with PTSD, OCD, or depression are more likely to experience panic attacks.
- **Genetic factors:** Some people's genetic makeup may be predisposed to developing emotional problems that could result in panic attacks.
- **The use of stimulants:** Some people may develop panic attacks when they abuse the use of stimulants such as amphetamines, caffeine, and cocaine.

What Keeps Panic Attacks Going?

CBT is always very concerned about what keeps a problem going. This is because if you can work out what keeps a problem going, then you can be able to treat it by interrupting the maintenance cycle. David Clark, a psychologist, identified the key maintenance process in panic attacks, and that is: people who experience panic tend to misinterpret the sensations of their body.

How Panic Attacks Develop

To understand how panic attack develops, take a look at the scenario below:

David notices he has a body sensation and says to himself, "my breathing feels cold," then he goes on to have a thought about it "could this be dangerous?" This thought then triggers and apprehensive feeling, which causes him to have anxiety about this feeling, thus strengthening the body sensations, making David to say to himself, "this is really bad." As David pays more attention to his bodily sensations, he becomes even more apprehensive about how he feels, resulting in having even more catastrophic thoughts such as "this is getting even worse," I think I'm going to pass out."

The outcome of this process is that David's misinterpretation of his body sensations would result in feelings of panic reaching its peak.

Other things people who suffer from panic does, which inadvertently prolong their panic disorder are:

- **Looking out for dangerous sensations of the body:** Keeping watch for body sensations is problematic because the more you pay attention to it, the more you are most likely going to experience it.

- **Misinterpreting your body sensations:** Harmless body sensations are most times mistaken to mean an impending catastrophe.
- **Avoiding feared situations or body sensations:** When you avoid situations or things that have to do with panic, it means you will never get to learn how to cope with them or how dangerous they really are. Avoiding situations associated with panic, or using safety behaviors with the intent to prevent a catastrophe are problematic because they not only maintain unhelpful panic-related beliefs but also fail to challenge it.
- **Safety-seeking behaviors:** Safety-seeking behaviors are things you do when you try to prevent a catastrophe from happening. Like avoidance, safety behaviors will prevent you from learning how well you could really cope or how dangerous that situation really is.

Treatment Options for Panic Attacks

One of the core treatment options for panic attacks/panic disorder is CBT, and the technique it uses is exposure therapy. In our previous discussions on how exposure therapy works, we touched on a number of areas to help us better understand how to use this technique in treating anxiety disorders effectively. I also briefly discussed the three major forms of exposure therapy, with each addressing a specific anxiety disorder. These forms are imaginary exposure, in-vivo exposure, and interoceptive exposure (please refer to the [section on exposure therapy](#) if you are yet to). Of these forms of therapy, interoceptive exposure is mostly used for panic attacks since it centers on controlling bodily or physical sensations. Hence, our focus would center around how you can use interoceptive exposure to effectively overcome panic attacks. Identifying cognitive distortions and cognitive restructuring are likewise used to treat panic attacks. Please refer to [Chapter 2](#) for an in-depth discussion on this treatment option, which is a golden standard for all types of conditions.

Interoceptive Exposure

As early discussed under the **Exposure Therapy** section of this book, interoceptive exposure requires you to be exposed to your feared bodily sensations to elicit the feared reaction, i.e., it will activate any unhelpful beliefs that are associated with the bodily sensations, maintains the sensations with no distraction or avoidance, and then allows new learning about the sensations to occur. Because the trigger for panic attacks in the context of panic disorder is the body, the focus of the exposure exercises is on the anxiety symptoms themselves. Thus, the goal of this technique is to help you not only see that the symptoms of panic are unharmful, though uncomfortable, but also to help you cope with your panic attacks and effectively put a stop to it.

Without further ado, let's take a look at how to put the exposure exercise into practice. But first, below are a number of interoceptive exposure exercises that you can use to toughen up against the probability of experiencing a panic attack. It is important that you practice one exercise daily after attempting a number of them to find the one that will trigger some anxiety. This is because each person may not respond the same way to the same exercise.

Symptom - Dizziness or lightheadedness

- Spin for 1 minute in a swivel chair, then take a 1 minute break. Repeat this 8 times.

- For 30 seconds, shake head from side to side, then take a 30 second break. Repeat this 15 times.

- Bend over and place head in-between the legs for 30 seconds while sitting, then quickly sit up. Repeat this 15 times.

- Hyperventilate (shallow breathing at a rate of 100-120 breaths per minute) for 1 minute, then breathe normally for another 1 minute. Repeat this 8 times.

Symptom - Derealization

- For 1 minute, stare at a light on the ceiling, then try reading for 1 minute. Repeat this 8 times.

- Stare at yourself in a mirror for 3 minutes, then one minute break. Repeat this 3 times.

- For 3 minutes, stare at a small dot (like the size of a dime) posted on the wall.

- For 2 minutes, stare at an optical illusion (such as a "psychedelic" rotating screen saver, rotating spiral, etc.), then break for one minute. Repeat this 5 times.

Symptom - Tightness in throat

Wear a scarf, tie, or turtleneck shirt tightly around your neck for 5 minutes, take 1 minute break. Repeat this 3 times.

Symptm - Rapid heartbeat

Run up and downstairs, or on the spot for 1 minute, then take a 1 minute break. Repeat this 8 times.

Symptom - Breathlessness or smothering feelings

- For 30 seconds, hold your breath, then breathe normally for another 30 seconds. Repeat this 15 times.

- For 2 minutes, breathe through a small narrow straw (plug your nose if necessary), then breathe normally for 1 minute. Repeat this 5 times.

- Sit with your head covered by a heavy blanket or coat.

Symptom - Choking feelings, gag reflex

For a few seconds or until a gag reflex is induced, place a tongue depressor or a smooth unharmful object such as a brush on the back of your tongue. Repeat this for 15 minutes.

Symptom - Trembling or shaking

For 60 seconds, tense all the muscles in your body or hold a push-up position for as long as you can, then break for another 60 seconds. Repeat this 8 times.

Symptom - Sweating

- Sit in a hot car, a hot, stuffy room, or a small room with a space heater)

- Take a hot drink

Using the interoceptive exercises above as well as the steps of systemic desensitization as discussed under the exposure therapy section, let's see what an interoceptive exposure for panic attacks would look like using the experience of Jane, who suffers from panic attacks.

Jane is a 30-year-old woman with a panic disorder. She experiences panic attacks that appear out of the blues, often worrying about having another panic attack episode. In some cases, she feels a little anxious, and starts to feel dizzy, thus making her worry the panic attack might get worse; and yes, it usually does. Jane decides to visit a therapist who immediately identified the interoceptive exposure exercise as one of the suitable treatment options to address the bodily sensations that cause her to panic. Below is a step by step process Jane underwent with the help of her therapist.

Step One: Pick a Trigger

To begin the exercise, Jane chooses to start with the "dizziness" trigger, because it is most often the body sensation that triggers the panicky thoughts fueling the anxiety and making it worse.

Step Two: Create a Fear Hierarchy

Using the list her therapist gave her, Jane went on to list the different interoceptive exercises that she can use to trigger some anxiety.

Exposure exercise (ways to trigger the anxiety)

- Spin for 1 minute in a swivel chair, then 1 minute break. Repeat this 8 times.

- For 30 seconds, shake head from side to side, then 30 second break. Repeat this 15 times.

- Bend over and place head in-between the legs for 30 seconds while sitting, then quickly sit up. Repeat this 15 times.

- Hyperventilate (shallow breathing at a rate of 100-120 breaths per minute) for 1 minute, then breathe normally for another 1 minute. Repeat this 8 times.

Step Three: Rate the Hierarchy

Using a scale of 0-10 (a Subjective Units of Distress Scale: SUDS), Jane rates the level of anxiety/distress about the sensations for each exercise, where 0 is the lowest, and 10 the highest.

Exposure Exercise	*Anxiety Rating*
- Spin for 1 minute in a swivel chair, Then take a 1 minute break. Repeat this 8 times.	7
- For 30 seconds, shake your head from side	9

to side, then 30 second break.
Repeat this 15 times.

- Bend over and place head in-between   7
the legs for 30 seconds while sitting,
then quickly sit up. Repeat this 15
times.

- Hyperventilate (shallow breathing at   5
a rate of 100-120 breaths per minute)
for 1 minute, then breathe normally
for another 1 minute. Repeat this 8 times

SUDS		
Rating	Meaning	Comment
0	Relaxed	You feel no distress. You feel calm.
1-4	Mild	You feel like you are more nervous or alert, but you can still cope.
5-6	Moderate	It is becoming difficult for you to cope with. You are distracted by anxiety and might use safety behaviors or avoidance.
7-8	High	It is difficult to cope with. You are having difficulties concentrating, and you are looking to escape.
9-10	Severe to extreme	You can't cope. The response of your body is extremely overwhelming that you think you cannot stay in the situation any longer.

Step Four: Starting Exposure

In the 5-6 range on the SUDS, Jane picks an exposure exercise item from the list. She begins her practice of hyperventilating for 1 minute, then takes a 1 minute break, repeating it 8 times – which takes her about 16 minutes to complete. Whenever she experiences severe fear of her panic attacks in the process of undertaking this exercise, she quickly practised the relaxation training skills she learned on deep breathing, which helped to lower her bodily anxiety response. She uses the SUDS to track her progress by rating her anxiety level before and after the exposure.

Step Five: Middle Sessions of Exposure

Once Jane feels like her anxiety level for the hyperventilation exercise has reduced to around a "3", she then moves to the next harder exercise on the hierarchy. She continues practising these exercises daily and keeps moving up the hierarchy until she gets accustomed to the feeling of lightheadedness or dizziness, as well as being more at peace with the probability that she might have a panic attack when she feels lightheaded or dizzy.

Since she is also worried when the feeling of tightness is experienced in her throat, Jane decided to go through some of the interoceptive exercises for this sensation as well. Jane and her therapist, along with her exposure practice, worked on some of the thoughts that tend to fuel the anxiety once it is triggered. Please refer to Chapter 2 on the section of identifying cognitive distortions and cognitive restructuring to learn more about how negative thoughts can be identified and reframed.

Step Six: Ending Exposure

Jane continues practising the exposure exercises for about 10 weeks, changing the exercise for about each week as she moved up the hierarchy. This, with a combination of cognitive skills, improved her panic symptoms and made her feel confident enough to manage a panic attack that might occur in the future.

Exercise

Following the steps Jane went through in confronting the body sensations that caused her to experience panic attacks, use the table below to document your journey. But before you begin, kindly pay attention to the following.

Precautions

It is essential that you take note of the following before attempting any of the exposure exercises.

1. You must be physically healthy before starting or completing the exercises. If you have any health challenges that might be complicated by the physical strain from the exercises, then you should either not take the exercise, or discontinue

the exercise, whichever comes first. Some of the health challenges include:

- Epilepsy or seizures
- A heart condition
- Pregnancy
- Physical injuries, e.g., neck problem
- History of fainting/ low blood pressure

Check with your therapist/ doctor to determine if you can proceed with the exposure exercises given your condition.

2. Although exposure exercises are typically performed with the guidance of a therapist or a mental health professional, conducting these exposure exercises on your own is most times the best way to challenge or confront your beliefs about body sensations. However, if you find any exercises particularly difficult, or you are concerned about your progress, please get in touch with a therapist or a licensed mental health practitioner to guide you through the process.

Preparation for the tasks

Ensure you try to trigger all the body sensations or symptoms using the interoceptive exercises highlighted underneath each sensation. This will help you determine which body sensations and exercises are relevant to you or that causes you to panic so that you know which of them to focus on.

Below are a few hints to help you as you prepare for the exercises.

1. Talking to a trusted or supportive friend or relative about the tasks you are doing can be helpful. Perhaps you can regularly talk with them to discuss your progress and if you are having any challenges. This can help you in acknowledging the positive steps being taken and can serve as a motivation for you to continue.

2. The exercises are not in any particular order. However, it is best you start with the exercises that have the lowest anxiety rating and gradually move up the hierarchy. This way, you won't be so overwhelmed and decide to use safety behaviors or avoidance to discontinue the exercise.

3. Write down which exercise(s) you will complete each day, and create an appointment to perform

the exercises by blocking out a time that is convenient for you on your calendar. This will help you in formalizing your commitment to doing it. Ensure that you set aside enough time to complete at least 1 exercise every day.

Performing the tasks

1. Experience the sensations as much as you can and avoid using safety behaviors or avoidance to distract yourself from the sensations. Take note of the ways you can subtly avoid these sensations. Common methods of avoidance include:

    - Stopping the task early. For instance, when you are thinking, "That's enough, my heart is beating faster."

    - Not properly completing the tasks. For instance, when you are attempting to trigger the sensation of sweating through heat, you partly open the window, which is a subtle form of avoidance.

    - Distracting yourself from paying attention to the sensations instead of paying full attention to them.

2. During the exercises, use disputation (refer to Chapter 2 on cognitive restructuring) to confront or challenge any catastrophic/ negative thoughts about the sensations you experience. Perhaps you can make a flashcard and have it close by.

3. Whenever you experience fear of panic attacks in the process of undergoing an exercise, quickly apply the relaxation training skills you learned to help you confront your fears and lower your bodily anxiety response.

4. Although experiencing some sensation is better than nothing, ensure you complete the full exercise – this will provide you with a more accurate assessment of the fear of your sensation.

5. In some exercises, the sensations can develop during the exercise, while in others, they develop shortly after the exercise. So, ensure you pay full attention to the sensations that take place during and after the exercise.

6. After each exercise, make some notes about your experience using SUDS.

Ongoing exposure

Working through an exposure session is very critical if you want to get used to the feared sensations. To keep moving onwards and upwards, below are a few hints to help you with the process of moving through all of your feared sensations.

- **Repetition:** It is important that you repeat each exercise until your SUDS rating decreases to less than 5. This can be done later on the same day, or you can have it scheduled for the next day or so.

- **Acknowledge your achievements:** After completing an exposure session, ensure that you reward yourself for your efforts. The reward should be something you find positive and encouraging in recognition of your achievements.

- **Use your resources:** Talk to a trusted relative or friend or even your therapist about your progress, and work through any unhelpful thoughts you might have concerning the completion of the exercises.

Exercise	Before Exercise SUDS (0-10)	After Exercise SUDS (0-10)	Symptoms & Thoughts What did you notice in your body? What went through your mind?
Dizziness or lightheadedness - Spin for 1 minute in a swivel chair, then take a 1 minute break. Repeat this 8 times. - For 30 seconds, shake your head from side to side, then 30 second break. Repeat this 15 times.			

- Bend over and place head in-between the legs for 30 seconds while sitting, then quickly sit up. Repeat this 15 times. - Hyperventilate (shallow breathing at a rate of 100-120 breaths per minute) for 1 minute, then breathe normally for another 1 minute. Repeat this 8 times.			
Derealization - For 1 minute, stare at a light on the ceiling, then try reading for 1 minute. Repeat this 8 times. - Stare at yourself in a mirror for 3 minutes, then one minute break.			

Repeat this 3 times. - For 3 minutes, stare at a small dot (like the size of a dime) posted on the wall. - For 2 minutes, stare at an optical illusion (such as a "psychedelic" rotating screen saver, rotating spiral, etc.), then break for one minute. Repeat this 5 times.			
Tightness in throat Wear a scarf, tie, or turtleneck shirt tightly around your neck for 5 minutes, take one minute break. Repeat this 3 times.			
Rapid heartbeat Run up and downstairs, or on the spot for 1 minute, then take a 1 minute break. Repeat this 8 times.			

Choking feelings, gag reflex For a few seconds or until a gag reflex is induced, place a tongue depressor or a smooth unharmful object such as a brush on the back of your tongue. Repeat this for 15 minutes.			
Trembling or shaking For 60 seconds, tense all the muscles in your body or hold a push-up position for as long as you can, then break for another 60 seconds. Repeat this 8 times.			
Sweating - Sit in a hot car, a hot, stuffy room, or a small room with a space heater) - Take a hot drink			

Breathlessness or smothering feelings			
- For 30 seconds, hold your breath, then breathe normally for another 30 seconds. Repeat this 15 times.			
- For 2 minutes, breathe through a small narrow straw (plug your nose if necessary), then breathe normally for 1 minute. Repeat this 5 times.			
- Sit with your head covered by a heavy blanket or coat.			

The end... almost!

Hey! We've made it to the final chapter of this book, and I hope you've enjoyed it so far.

If you have not done so yet, I would be incredibly thankful if you could take just a minute to leave a quick review on the product page of this book.

Reviews are not easy to come by, and as an independent author with a little marketing budget, I rely on you, my readers, to leave a short review on the product page of this book

Even if it is just a sentence or two!

So if you really enjoyed this book, please... leave a brief review on the product page of this book.

I truly appreciate your effort to leave your review, as it truly makes a huge difference.

Thanks once again from the depth of my heart for purchasing this book and reading it to the end.

Chapter 5

CBT for Anger Management

What is Anger?

Anger is a natural response to threats that can either inspire us to confront injustice or problematic situations or can motivate us to protect ourselves when attacked. The fact is, everyone gets angry, and this is normal. However, there is a need for us to manage our anger. Common sense and social norms tell us that we cannot lash out each time we get irritated or upset.

Anger varies in intensity, i.e., what causes one person to be mildly irritated might trigger an intense rage in someone else. Similarly, people express anger differently. While some verbally express their anger by shouting, swearing, name-calling, or making threats, others become violent by hitting or pushing others or even by breaking things they lay their hands on. Also, some people express their anger in passive ways, for instance, by sulking or ignoring others. Other people may bottle up when they feel very angry or even turn it against themselves by self-harming.

At this point, I need to mention that anger and aggression are not one and the same. While anger is an emotion that we feel, aggression, on the other hand, is the behavior that, in some cases, stems from the thoughts and feelings of anger. In other words, you can be angry but choose not to be aggressive.

Angry Thoughts, Behaviors, and Physical Symptoms

Anger tends to be associated with the thoughts of hostility, maladaptive behaviors, and physiological arousal. Thoughts most times, focuses on the perceived rights and wrongs and a feeling or sense of injustice (such as 'I'm being disrespected'; 'I'm badly/unfairly treated,' 'I'm being disappointed again,' 'They're making a mockery of me' etc.). In other cases, it is often a sense that others have fallen short of your expectations, or standards (such as 'This isn't good enough'; 'I won't accept this,' 'I can't trust anyone' etc.).

The physical consequence of anger is that it results in physiological changes. Your blood pressure and heart rate go up, and your adrenaline level rises. Anger can also impair your concentration and memory capability.

Other physical symptoms that are noticeable from an angry person include teeth or fist clenching, stomach-churning/butterflies, tense muscles, and shaking, amongst others.

When angry, you might feel restless, on edge, tense, or uptight. You might also feel the urge to hit out, ignore or not talk to a person, shout or argue, make sarcastic comments, or even storm away from a situation.

The Cycle of Anger – How Anger Develops

An episode of anger display begins from ground zero and gradually builds up, or rapidly via three stages. Here we will discuss these stages alongside the actions associated with them.

- **Escalation** – At this stage, you begin to receive several cues our mind and body alert us to about the build-up of anger from the inside. These cues include physical (heavy breathing), cognitive (thoughts of revenge), emotional (guilt), or behavioral (teeth-clenching).
- **Expression** – Should the phase of escalation go unattended, the expression phase will follow suit shortly. A violent display of anger is

characterized by this, which may include physical or verbal aggression.

- **Post-expression** – At this stage, you begin to realize the negative consequences of your physical or verbal aggressiveness. This could be inner feelings of guilt, regret, shame to external consequences such as retribution, or arrest from others.

Everyone has his/ her personal intensity, duration, and frequency of anger in the anger cycle. For instance, someone may get angry in just a few minutes, while another may escalate gradually with time before hitting the expression stage. The goal of CBT is to prevent anyone from reaching the expression stage. With the use of CBT techniques and practices, anger can be identified and managed before it reaches the escalation stage.

Causes of Anger

- **Family background**: People who easily get angry may come from a chaotic or difficult family background. They may have never been encouraged nor learned to express how they feel healthily. A person who is/ was emotionally deprived (for example, not being nurtured when young, or not receiving empathy) and punitive parenting (being frequently shamed, invalidated, or criticized) can lead to low self-esteem, mistrust, and anger.

- **Negative thinking style**: Difficult situations or events can lead to a negative thinking style, which then becomes ingrained with time and becomes a part of one's outlook on life. Negative thinking can turn into a bad habit, so much that you are not aware your thinking style is becoming excessively negative and how it is affecting your day-day life. Unsurprisingly, a continuous negative outlook can result in anger problems.

- **Low tolerance for frustration:** Some people laugh off or forget about minor frustrations from everyday life (such as traffic jams, a poor internet, or phone connection, unfriendly shopkeepers, etc.), and others find it difficult letting go and may even end up fuming hours later. People who get angry easily tend to have what is called a low tolerance for frustration. One's genes and environment/ upbringing are factors that can influence if you have a low tolerance for frustration. Frustrations are part and parcel of life, so toughening up your tolerance level is an essential part of anger management.

- **Stress:** Stressful life events such as abuse or being bullied, divorce, or separated, financial problems, work pressures, and job loss can drive one to anger.

Cost of Anger

- Some people think 'letting it all out' is a good way of getting the anger out of their system. Studies show that doing so, in fact, does escalate the anger and aggression levels.

- Anger hurts relationships, whether it is family, romantic, friendship, or professional. 'You are always messing things up!' 'This damn machine does not work,' – these types of black-and-white statements can upset and alienate the person who hears them, thereby making them less inclined to help you.

- Anger disrupts your thinking patterns. Instead of trying to resolve problems calmly, anger exaggerates them. This can briefly fortify your self-esteem and make you feel your anger is justified, but ultimately, it fosters feelings of hopelessness, making resolvable problems seem unresolvable.

- People most times feel very badly about themselves after having an angry outburst, resulting in feelings of guilt and shame.

Myths & Facts About Anger

Several widespread beliefs and myths exist concerning anger. Let's deconstruct these myths to see what the facts are.

Myth 1 – Venting out my anger relaxes me. It isn't healthy holding it in.

Fact – Holding on to anger is like you holding in your palms red-hot coals. Anger should be expressed, but not by being aggressive because aggressiveness will only result in further confrontations.

Myth 2 – My aggressive behavior gives me the attention, obedience, and respect I deserve

Fact – Understanding someone and not by intimidation lies the power to influence. People may submit to you out of being bullied, but they won't give you the respect you seek, and eventually, you will be deserted if you are unable to accept opposing viewpoints.

Myth 3 – I cannot control my anger.

Fact – Anger, like any other emotion, is also a result of the situation you are in. Assessing the situation from multiple perspectives prevents misjudgment and anger.

Myth 4 – Suppressing your anger is all about anger management.

Fact – Anger is neither to be suppressed nor vented out, instead, it should be expressed in a manner that is non-violent and constructive. This is what Anger Management is all about.

CBT Treatment for Anger

CBT teaches us that how we behave when we are angry depends on our ability to manage our feelings and express our emotions.

In cognitive behavioral therapy, your therapist will:

- Help you understand the events/ situations and your interpretations of those situations that led to your feelings of anger.

- Help you in identifying possible distortions in how you think about a situation, and challenge you to uncover the validity of these distortions.

- Help you to reframe the thoughts into more balanced and adaptive ("cool") thoughts.

To achieve the above, I would use the Albert Ellis A-B-C-D technique, who is credited as one of the pioneers of CBT. This technique employs the use of thought records in challenging distorted or irrational thinkings about a situation and reconstructing them into more realistic and rational ones.

Another well-known technique is relaxation training, which includes deep breathing, progressive muscle relaxation, and mindfulness, all of which are proven methods in managing anger. In chapter 4 of this book, I discussed the relaxation training technique. Kindly refer to this section if you haven't yet done so.

Ellis's A-B-C-D Technique

The A-B-C-D model is a classic CBT technique which, when applied effectively, can help in addressing several emotional difficulties, including anger management problems. In chapter 1 of this book, I briefly touched on this model as a type of CBT. However, I would go deeper into explaining how this model can be applied to anger management.

Below is an overview of what the A-B-C-D model looks like, using anger as the problem focus:

A = Activating Event

This is the situation or trigger that stirs up your anger.

B = Belief System

This refers to your interpretation of the activating event (A) such as *"What are your beliefs and expectations of other people's behavior?" "What is it you tell yourself about what occurred?"* In chapter 2 of this book, I discussed the belief system extensively and how to identify your core beliefs about a situation/ problem. Please refer to this chapter if you are yet to do so.

C = Consequences

This refers to how you feel and what you do per your belief system, i.e., the emotional and behavioral consequences resulting from A + B. When angry, it is also typical to feel other emotions such as fear. Other consequences that may arise include clenching your fists, feeling warm, and taking more shallow breaths. More dramatic behavioral consequences include name-calling, yelling, and physical violence.

D = Dispute

This is a critical step in the anger management process. This requires that you examine your belief system and expectations. This step helps you question if your beliefs and expectations are unrealistic or irrational? And if so, what would a calmer and alternative way to relate to the situation be? By disputing those knee-jerk beliefs, you can then begin to take a more rational and balanced approach toward the situation, which can help you control your anger.

In summary, this step aims to identify cognitive distortions in your thinking and how it can be restructured into more balanced thoughts. I discussed extensively on this in Chapter 2. You can refer to this chapter for more in-depth details. However, in this section, using an example, I would discuss as clearly as possible how to identify distorted or unrealistic thinking and how to dispute your distorted thoughts or expectations and reframe them into more realistic ones.

Example of the A-B-C-D Model

Let's take a look at an example as I describe how this model can be applied to anger management.

A = Activating Event

You are driving to work, and you get cut off by somebody, almost resulting in a collision. To begin with, you were already feeling worn out because you were running late to work and had a big day ahead of you.

B = Belief System

You think to yourself, "people should not drive in such a way like that," "I'm a very courteous driver, and I don't drive like that," "every driver on the road these days are reckless," "if I had been hit by that car, I would have been so late to work, or it could have been even worse, I could have gotten injured."

C = Consequences

After the event that triggered your beliefs (i.e., being cut-off in traffic), you then rolled down your window and exploded in anger at the other driver. You observe your muscles becoming tensed, your heart beats rapidly, and you feel like hitting the steering wheel. You also notice you feel some elements of fear.

D = Dispute

In responding to the situation that triggered your anger, instead of reinforcing the thoughts that fuel your anger, you could instead, reconstruct your thinking (this is the dispute part of the model). For instance, you could say to yourself:

"It is disappointing that some people drive so recklessly, but that is just how life is. Most people actually do adhere to road safety rules, and I'm glad I do as well. Probably that driver had an emergency he was responding to, or probably not, but you'll never know. It was scary to have almost gotten hit. Still, even if we got into a fender bender, I would have,

nonetheless, gotten to work, and probably nothing serious would have occurred because of it."

As you can see, applying this type of rational thinking and self-talk is most likely going to diffuse some of the anger and help you relax and remain calm.

Although using the A-B-C-D model is a good practice even though it is after the fact, it is, however, reflective of the process that helps to rewire your brain and retrain your mind by increasing your awareness of patterns in your thoughts and the situations, and ways you can respond to them more effectively. For example, you may begin noticing that there are similar situations that constantly bring up anger for you. Essentially, these are areas of vulnerability you need to be aware of and work hard on.

Most times, after an angry incident, people get insight into what just happened and regretting what they said or did. But, at the time, things just happen to escalate so quickly. This added level of awareness can really help you slow down a bit – a key factor in anger management. Being able to take a pause, breathe deeply, and then deciding how to respond instead of reacting to the situation can help prevent the negative consequences of your anger.

P.S: The ABCD model in the context described above can likewise be applied to depression and anxiety disorders.

Exercise

Using the ABCD Model to Manage Your Anger

The first step toward using this anger management tool is by increasing your awareness of what is going on in each step. To begin this exercise, review each of the following:

- Identify what situation or event that triggered your anger.

- Reflect on your beliefs/ response to the triggering situation (e.g., what did you say about it to yourself).

- Identify all the emotional and behavioral responses that ensued.

Because our minds are fast-paced, we can get to the consequence C very quickly. So, to begin applying this model, it would also be helpful that you do some analyses of previous situations that have triggered your anger by noting them down in each category. To help you with this task, use the thought record below:

A = Activating Agent	B = Beliefs	C = Consequence	D = Dispute
The situation or trigger that made you angry	Your interpretation of the trigger; what you say about it to yourself	How you felt and what you did about your response to your beliefs; the emotional and behavioral consequences from A + B	Examine your beliefs and expectations. Are they irrational or unrealistic? If so, what other ways can you relate to the situation

Taking your time to write out these steps can really help you in getting this learning into your subconscious mind so that you can draw upon it later on in the heat of the moment. In other words, doing this can help with your practice of anger management, especially when reviewing previous incidents and coming up with more balanced and positive solutions that can help in calming you down, instead of fueling the anger.

After writing down the A-B-Cs, complete the D-dispute section by identifying more rational, realistic, and balanced things you can rather say to yourself about the situation. Likewise, you can include specific behaviors in this section. For instance, you might want to write down reminders as a note to yourself, such as "count to 10 before making any utterances" or "take some deep breaths."

Conclusion

I'd like to thank and congratulate you for transiting the lines of this book from start to finish.

I hope this book helped in providing you with a clearer understanding of what cognitive behavioral therapy (CBT) is all about and how important this therapeutic approach can be to your mental health and emotional wellbeing. In this book, I showed factual evidence to support the effectiveness of CBT in treating several health conditions that include depression, anxiety, anger, and panic attacks and likewise, I discussed to a great extent the proven CBT techniques you can apply right away to get your mental health and overall wellbeing in the right state and shape. These techniques in no particular order include how to identify distortions in your thinking and how to challenge and replace them with more rational thoughts, how to use behavioral activation to overcome depression, how to use exposure therapy to end anxiety, how to use relaxation training skills such as deep breathing and mindfulness, and specifically, how to use interoceptive exposure therapy to stop panic attacks in its tracks. I also showed you how to use the A-B-C-D technique to manage your anger and get your emotions under control. Above all else and most importantly, I hope that you found these techniques to be quite insightful and useful either as a therapist seeking additional knowledge in your profession or as someone looking for ways to exercise control over his/her mental health.

At this point onward, you are now equipped to lend better therapeutic advice to your patient or able to take better control of your health. The next step is to apply the techniques discussed, which this book has demonstrated as invaluable. So, I urge you to feel free to experiment with these techniques right away without hesitation. Personally, most of what I have shared and discussed were the steps I took toward reclaiming my health from when I was once depressed, anxious, and angry about everything, and because I know how powerful these techniques were in helping me break the hold these vicious emotions had on me, I too want you to break the hold they have on you or your patient.

Finally, I want you to take personal responsibility for your health and wellbeing by incorporating the tips I have shared in this book into your daily life routine. No one can do this for you, except you.

Remember...

"Knowing is not enough; we must apply. Willing is not enough; we must do" – Goethe.

I wish you the very best on your journey toward health and wellness!

References

Whalley, M. H. K. (2020, July 5). What is Cognitive Behavioral Therapy (CBT)? Retrieved from https://www.psychologytools.com/self-help/what-is-cbt/

Ben Martin, P., 2020. In-Depth: Cognitive Behavioral Therapy. Psych Central. Available at: <https://psychcentral.com/lib/in-depth-cognitive-behavioral-therapy/>

Suffolkcognitivetherapy.com. 2020. Types Of CBT | Suffolk Cognitive-Behavioral, PLLC. Available at: <http://suffolkcognitivetherapy.com/web/specialties/types-of-cbt/>

Whalley, M. H. K. (2020b, July 5). What is Cognitive Behavioral Therapy (CBT)? Retrieved from https://www.psychologytools.com/self-help/what-is-cbt/

Eddins, R. M. (2020, June 19). Feeling Anxious or Depressed? Watch Out for Cognitive Distortions.

Retrieved from https://eddinscounseling.com/types-of-cognitive-distortions/

Grohol, J. P. M. (2020, July 6). Depression. Retrieved from https://psychcentral.com/depression/

Williams, A. (2015, July 9). Core Beliefs Part 1: Identifying and Understanding Core Beliefs. Retrieved from https://www.rowancenterla.com/new-blog/2015/7/9/core-beliefs-part-1-identifying-and-understanding-core-beliefs

Psychology Tools. 2020. Delivering More Effective Exposure Therapy In CBT - Psychology Tools. Available at:<https://www.psychologytools.com/articles/delivering-more-effective-exposure-therapy-in-cbt/>

Eddins, R. M. (2020b, June 19). Identifying and Changing Your Core Beliefs | Learn How CBT Can Help. Retrieved from https://eddinscounseling.com/uncover-core-beliefs-can-change/

Therapy, H. (2019, October 19). Core Beliefs in CBT - Identifying And Analysing Personal Beliefs. Retrieved from https://www.harleytherapy.co.uk/counselling/core-beliefs-cbt.htm

Cognitive behavioral therapy in anxiety disorders: current state of the evidence. (2011, December 1). Retrieved from https://www.ncbi.nlm.nih.gov/pmc/articles/PMC3263389/

Grohol, J. P. M. (2020a, July 6). Anxiety Disorders. Retrieved from https://psychcentral.com/anxiety/

Treated, P. and management, A., 2020. CBT Cork | Anger Management.| Kinsale CBT. Available at: <https://www.kinsalecbt.com/anger-management/>

Pratt, K. L. (2017, May 12). Psychology Tools: A-B-C-D Model for Anger Management. Retrieved from https://healthypsych.com/psychology-tools-a-b-c-d-model-for-anger-management/

www.ingramcontent.com/pod-product-compliance
Lightning Source LLC
Chambersburg PA
CBHW051524020426
42333CB00016B/1772